Praise for My Checkered Life: A Marriage Memoir

"MY CHECKERED LIFE: A MARRIAGE MEMOIR is honest, big-hearted, nonjudgmental, humorous, and wise. Not a book of easy answers, Beaman doesn't gloss over hard truths. Instead, she shares personal examples acknowledging that marriage, like a rollercoaster ride, has ups and downs that can plummet us from calm to chaos, despair to joy, and everything in between. I laughed, and I cried, and you will, too."

– Laurie Buchanan, PhD., author *Note to Self: A Seven-Step Path to Gratitude and Growth*

"Like a finely-made quilt, this memoir snatches the leftovers and used materials of life and transforms them into a dazzling heirloom. Marian Beaman and her husband Cliff, appear on these pages as young lovers, parents, artists, teachers, and elders. Those of us who are faithful readers of Marian's blog and her first memoir *Mennonite Daughter,* will love this book because we already know and love the main characters. However, we are like new readers, because the pattern of the quilt, and Cliff's fine contributions, have made the stories new."

– Shirley Hershey Showalter, author, *Blush*; co-author with Marilyn McEntyre, *The Mindful Grandparent*
shirleyshowalter.com

"This memoir evoked both laughter and tears. It caused me to evaluate my own relationships as I experienced the peaks and valleys of life with Marian and Cliff. Although the author and her husband come from different backgrounds, they have one thing in common: they made the decision to be faithful to each other. Because of this, they are able to love and forgive, to work together in spite of their imperfections."

– Elfrieda Neufeld Schroeder, PhD; Freelance Writer, Translator, Tutor, (ESL, German, English)

"Hilarious in places and real-to-life throughout, *My Checkered Life,* Marian Beaman's sequel to her memoir, *Mennonite Daughter,* gives an insider look at what makes her fifty-five-year marriage tick. Growing up as a plain Mennonite girl, English teacher from the East marries off-beat pioneer-type from the West and sparks fly, sometimes igniting arguments; other times finding harmony. Discover how their early commitment is tested but sustained by mutual love and trust."

– Melodie Miller Davis, author of *Memoir of an Unimagined Career* and nine other books. She is a newspaper columnist and blogs at findingharmonyblog.com.

Praise for My Checkered Life: A Marriage Memoir

"The first time I read *My Checkered Life*, I savored it slowly, but not too slowly, because the pages turned quickly as the stories flowed with ease. Not many people--wives or husbands--are brave enough to chronicle their marriage, including the ups and downs, the twisty turns of staying "in love" with a person through all of life's thick and thins.

The second time I read the book, I shared quotes and snippets with my husband, and we smiled knowingly. Marian Beaman does a spectacular job of detailing her move from innocent Mennonite young woman who yearns to be "fancy," to a woman in her mid-20s who falls for a man so different from her in many ways. And then, we follow their marriage from storybook wedding to the reality of living on a shoestring and traveling in a tiny travel trailer with small children and learning how to pay attention to their own needs, as well as to each other's. A beautiful testament (with heartfelt advice) on how to create and sustain a long-time, happy marriage."

– Pamela S. Wight, author *Flashes of Life*, blogger and teacher

My Checkered Life: A Marriage Memoir

Marian Longenecker Beaman

Copyright © 2023 Spindletree Books, Jacksonville, Florida. All rights reserved. Except for brief quotations in critical articles or reviews, no part of this book may be reproduced in any manner without prior written permission from the publisher. Includes bibliographical references.

All scripture texts quoted refer to the King James Version of the Bible, unless otherwise indicated.

While the author has confirmed that the references to website addresses (URLs) were accurate at the time of writing, URLs may have expired or changed since the manuscript was prepared.

Cover design: Cliff Beaman Graphics

Print ISBN 978-1-7335852-2-4

eBook ISBN 978-1-7335852-3-1

https://marianbeaman.com

My Checkered Life

A Marriage Memoir

Marian Longenecker Beaman

Spindletree Books

Dedication

To my husband Cliff, the Care Bear,
who has read every story I have written.
He has crafted the cover, designed the layout,
created original artwork and
restored photographs for this volume.

Contents

Introduction: How to Make an American Quilt   14

Part 1: Heritage and Home

1	How We Met	19
2	Tale of the Green Robe	31
3	Recipes: Viola Beaman and Ruth Longenecker	37
4	Viola Beaman's Shoulder Bag and Bossler's Sewing Circle	43
5	Grandma Fannie Longenecker: Artifacts and Diary	47
6	Aunt Ruth Longenecker: Autograph Book and Diaries	57
7	Cliff's Early School Days and Marian's Preschool	73
8	My Two Mothers	83
9	Mother and Daughter Define Beauty	87
10	Beamans and Longeneckers Socialize with Relatives	93

Part 2: Marital Happiness and Hassles

11	Our Wedding: The Mothers Meet	103
12	Marriage Ceremony	107
13	The Engagement: A Flashback	115
14	Wedding Guests and the Reception	125
15	Our Honeymoon and Camping in the Smokies	133
16	Change and Challenge	145
17	The Nomadic Family	155
18	Night of Crisis	161
19	Sad Friday: The Story of Daffodils	175
20	It's Not that Easy Being Green	181
21	A Toilet Tissue Tale, Ukraine Style	189

Part 3: Hilarity and High Emotion

22	My Husband's Humor	199
23	My Marriage in Vacuum Cleaners	203
24	Explosion in the Curio Cabinet	207
25	Conehead Confession	213
26	Where's My Spyglass?	217
27	Lunatic in London	225
28	Meet Me Under the Bougainvillea	235
29	Slights and Offenses: How Do You Handle Them?	241
30	Flash in the Pan: A Sunday Morning Argument	251
31	Finances: The Mislaid One Hundred Dollars & More	259

Part 4: Harmony in Marriage and in Life

32	Morning Ablution: What's Your Routine?	273
33	Moving the Body: Finding Balance	279
34	Lessons from the Bisque Salt and Pepper Shakers	283
35	Are You Too Big for Your Pot?	289
36	My Work is Loving the World	295
37	When Marian Subscribed to the Hustler Channel	303
38	Compensation: A Wedding Anniversary Meditation	309
39	Standing on the Promises: A Golden Anniversary	315
40	Marriage on the Rocks	321

Epilogue	333
References	339
Acknowlegements	345
About the Author	349
About the Artist	351

Preface

My Checkered Life is a sequel to my memoir, *Mennonite Daughter: The Story of a Plain Girl*. This new book offers a portrait of the highs and lows of a woman, wife, and mother who's curious about the world and the people in it. Discover what happened when I, at age twenty-six, married the man whose first portrait of me was a spoof: a goofy cartoon elephant with a blue bow around its tail.

Read this book with friends, and then gather with them to discuss questions posed at the end of each story.

Introduction:
How to Make an American Quilt

Finn isn't crazy about getting married. In the movie *How to Make an American Quilt*, Finn Dodd, a Berkeley graduate student, visits her great aunt and grandmother. She intends to finish her thesis and mull over a marriage proposal. Among her grandmother's sister and friends, Finn, played by actor Winona Ryder, learns that love can "sour, thicken, betray," even grow stronger. She also learns a thing or two about quilting from the women in a circle, stitching pieces of fabric together, blending disparate snippets to create beauty.

The movie, based on Whitney Otto's novel by the same name, also stars Anna (Maya Angelou), the organizer of the group, who chides Finn, "You have to choose your combinations careful. The right choices will enhance your quilt. The wrong choices will dull the colors and hide their original beauty. There are no rules you can follow. You have to go by instinct and you have to be brave."

Quilts can be fabric models of life with recurring motifs—but sometimes with new patterns. Since 2013, I have been "quilting" on my blog, *Plain and Fancy*, assembling pieces of Cliff's and my family heritage and highlights from our life together, including travel. These stories have inspired the themes in this book: Heritage and Home, Happiness and Hassles, Hilarity and High Emotion, and finally, moments of Harmony.

As I began writing this memoir, I assembled stories by following my fancy. My memory of family history or journal entries sometimes prompted my choice of themes. Sometimes, I didn't know how my stories would end, how the conclusion would evolve. Taking a walk in the preserve, soaking in my bathtub, or chatting with a friend often summoned the next best step. Sometimes my narrative came together without conscious thought. Often, like a quilter, I let instinct guide me. I just went with the flow.

I hope you can identify with my secrets and my struggles as a woman and wife, relate to my hassles, laugh at my memories of hilarity, and recall moments of harmony in your own life. After all, each of us is a "quilter" in our unique way as we "stitch" together the patterns in our own checkered lives, learning courage by taking risks, and—above all—embracing hope.

My Checkered Life: A Marriage Memoir

Part 1

Heritage and Home

"We all grow up with the weight of history on us. Our ancestors dwell in the attics of our brains as they do in the spiraling chains of knowledge hidden in every cell of our bodies."

– Shirley Abbott

My Checkered Life: A Marriage Memoir

Chapter 1

How We Met

A tiny tingle radiated from my heart to my hands when I read these lines: "Get thee out of thy country, and from thy kindred, and from thy father's house, unto a land that I will show you." This special verse, Genesis 12:1, is dated July 1966 in the margin of a Bible I still own. What I took as a command is the catalyst for change I refer to constantly as I planned the journey alone from Pennsylvania Dutch country to Charlotte, North Carolina. There I would begin a new and culturally shocking part of my life.

After graduating from Eastern Mennonite College in Virginia, I spent the last year and a half as Sister Longenecker, teacher of English to seniors at Lancaster Mennonite School. I watched my p's and q's inside and outside of the classroom, especially outside of the classroom, making sure the fabrics I bought at Musser's Fabric Shop to make my long, caped dresses were not too bright (maroon, not cherry red) and that I'm shod with pedestrian-looking shoes, brown or black–and *not* shiny patent leather, which I craved. In other words, I had to be a role model for my students.

My Checkered Life: A Marriage Memoir

My colleagues Verna, June and I shared experiences and expenses in a smallish trailer nestled in a grove of oaks on the edge of the campus. We risked renting a TV for major events (Kennedy's assassination, for example) and got caught once by an inquisitive student who knocked on our door, spied the blue glow of the TV, and reported us to the dean. The Dean Noah Good gently chided us to get our news by less worldly means, like the newspaper.

Life was calm and predictable like the repetitive blip on a heart monitor or the gentle swing of a clock pendulum. Too calm, in fact. I was ripe for change. My next-door neighbor, Paul, was dating a Guatemalan beauty, Betty, whom he met at Bob Jones University, considered the most square university in the world. I remember reading that information in the October 1965 issue of *Atlantic Monthly*. Paul showed me Cliff Beaman's photo in his yearbook, and the image grinned back at me like a clown. Paul told me Cliff is from the West Coast and doesn't want to spend ten days of his Christmas holiday in a car (actually a commodious, ancient hearse, I discover later) with eight other Westerners just to be home for Christmas. "Will you be Cliff's date for the holidays?" Paul proposed.

A few days before Christmas, I met the mystery man.

Thick, dark brown braids circle the back of my head like a slipped halo, held in place by black wire hairpins. The white net prayer veiling usually covering my head is missing this evening: I am beginning to chafe under the traditions set by my religious culture. Later in the evening. Paul, Betty, Cliff, and

1 – How We Met

I are all going out for a snack at the Plain and Fancy Restaurant. The doorbell rings at the Longenecker home. I wondered what Cliff looks like in person. And so, I meet him for the first time, he at the bottom and I at the top of the stairs leading down to the dining room and the entryway of our front door.

A tall, blond fellow with deep-set eyes looks up at me after Mom opens the door.

"Nice to see you *again*," Cliff says. *Oh, he's witty, I think.*

"Nice to see you again too," I say, not skipping a beat.

As the evening progresses, I find out that Cliff is an artist, and when he and I come back from the restaurant, I pose in the living room for my first live portrait. Several times I try to peek but to no avail.

"No," he insists, "it's not finished yet."

After thirty minutes of fierce sketching, he announces that the masterpiece is finished.

"Are you ready?" Cliff smiles, handing me my likeness. Shocked, I stare with open mouth and then blink in disbelief as he hands me a cartoon elephant with a blue ribbon around its tail.

"I can't imagine why you spent all this time on . . . just an elephant. Why didn't you draw a real picture of me?" Now, he laughs, a real guffaw.

Thus, I meet a blond, blue-eyed Christian clown who seems clever, likes art, and thinks (though he doesn't tell me then, of course) that I am the most unusual-looking woman he's ever met. There is mutual fascination: a young man from Washington state who wears a class ring the size of the Pope's, and a quaint-looking, plain girl from Lancaster County, Pennsylvania.

One evening a few days later the four of us, Paul, Betty, Cliff and I, pack ourselves into Paul's ancient, black Mercedes to go decorate the former Schwanger's Carpet Barn for Christmas This was before it became a mission of Rheems Grace Brethren Church. I say *pack ourselves* because Cliff and I are sharing the back seat with Paul's huge accordion case.

1 – How We Met

Cliff, I notice, is wearing a thick coat with a furry collar and a black Cossack hat; he looks bear-ish, for sure. Patches of recent snow dot the cold, hard ground creating a winter-scape that matches my somber mood. Just today the mail brought me a *Dear John* letter from a beau actually named John, a quasi-romantic carryover from college days. "I don't think we should continue our relationship," he says. Just like that! I have mixed feelings about this; I didn't actually like John all that much, but it was nice to have *someone* to date.

Cliff, Paul, and Betty are in high spirits as we tumble out of the car, loaded with boxes of holiday festoon: rolls of garland and tree decorations. I soon get carried along with their bright mood. We unfurl the green and red garland around the windows and trim the tree, activities I relish for the first time. Mennonite families of the sixties frowned upon the glitter and glitz of Christmas. When the church looks festive enough, Cliff gets out Paul's accordion and bellows, "Joo-eey to the Worr-ld, the Lor-rd is Come!" and we all join in. After a while, Paul and Betty practice the ever more joyous, "Ring the Bells." Betty's solo soprano is accompanied by Paul who loves to embellish her lyrical voice with lots of runs and trills.

Meanwhile, Cliff in the rear, is sketching on the chalkboard a Santa Claus, a snowman, and finally a manger scene.

He is really talented, I observe, but then wonder, *Why is he a theology student if he's so good in art?*

My Checkered Life: A Marriage Memoir

We're all getting hungry and Paul suggests, "Hey, let's go back home and make popcorn, eat peanut brittle and listen to records." Paul has a huge stash of LP's: Mantovani and *Reader's Digest* mood music: "Candlelight and Wine," "Heavenly Voices," "Hawaiian Paradise," and "Songs at Twilight." The Christmas tree lights at his house are all the illumination we'll need to fall into a sentimental mood.

And so, we pack up and climb back in the Mercedes with Cliff and me in the back seat again. The accordion case seems even more gigantic now, and there simply isn't room for all the arms and legs. "Excuse me, but I'm going to have to put my arm on the seat around you," Cliff says.

I think, *Oh, he doesn't want me to think that he's too forward.*

As the car moves deftly over the icy spots, thoughts of the *Dear John* letter fly into my head again, and I tell Cliff my sad news. My new-found friend seems to care genuinely. Tears fall and etch a crease down my face. He leans over to plant an empathetic kiss on my cheek, but misses the mark as I drop my head. Gentle as a butterfly, he touches my right eye with his lips instead.

How odd, I think. *A first kiss... and on my eye... how strange!*

Many nights Cliff and I indulge ourselves in the bounty of Paul's kitchen pantry. This upstairs kitchen is purposely stocked by his mom, Edna, who also happens to own the Clearview Diner on Route 230. On the nights we eat at the Clearview, we enjoy

1 – How We Met

Clearview Diner Elizathtoown, Pennsylvania

good Old Pennsylvania Dutch meals–chipped beef and creamed gravy slathered over toast, loads of meat loaf, potato salad, carrot and raisin salad, and heavenly desserts like banana pudding, Dutch apple pie, mince pie, all savored as we share bits and pieces from each other's lives.

And every night, it seems that we end of up again in Paul's tiny upstairs living room cramped by a large sofa. The lights from the tree which sits snugly in one corner seem to shimmer along with the strains of "Winter Wonderland." We find a tune that Cliff says is our song: "La Strada," the theme song from a Fellini drama, both comical and sad about man's loneliness and need for love. A recording of this song enjoys its place on my iPod to this day.

As we talk, the evening hours too soon fade into early morning. During these hours of popcorn, hot mulled cider, music and talk, our new bond of friendship grows quickly. We exchange stories about ourselves and our families, our hopes and ideals, and dreams of the future.

One evening I notice a button missing from Cliff's black "bear" coat and offer to sew it on. He digs around in his pocket and comes up with the button. Up and down, up and down, I sew and finally the button is snugly fastened to the wool jacket. I tie a knot on the underside and Cliff offers: "Here, let me cut the knot," as I hold the threads taut.

"Okay," I say, assured that he'll know what to do next. And then he snips the thread *under* the knot, totally severing it from the button.

"My stars," I scream incredulously, "What did you do that for? Now the button won't stay on because the knot is cut off!" I can't imagine how anyone wouldn't know where to snip the thread.

"Well, I didn't think I was actually cutting the knot off; I guess I just happened to cut too low," Cliff adds lamely.

But no excuse, logical or not, will suffice for what is in my books such an irresponsible mistake. The discussion escalates to a one-sided argument, and only a kiss temporarily diffuses the dismay I feel. My anger spent, Cliff then leans over, kisses me on the mouth this time. "I think I'm falling in *like*," he whispers in my ear.

1 – How We Met

Cliff and Marian holding up watercolor

Never before had I dated a man who wasn't Mennonite. "Beaman" certainly wasn't a family name I heard in Lancaster County where I grew up, or at Eastern Mennonite College, which back then attracted many students from Ohio, Indiana, Pennsylvania, and Virginia, where the college was located. Cliff, this strange man, was a Westerner, having lived in California, Washington, and Idaho. Fortunately, a year earlier my Mennonite friend Joann Herr invited me to tour forty-seven states in our country, introducing me to tall sequoias, redwoods, the vast expanse of desert, and the majestic Rockies. Now I had some idea what our country looked like beside the farmlands of Lancaster County, Pennsylvania or the purple mountains bordering Virginia's Shenandoah Valley.

A few days after I met the man I would one day marry, Cliff mentioned his family. Twenty-two-year-old college students don't usually carry family photos in their wallets. So, Cliff went into detail, describing his younger two sisters, Joyce and Kathy still living at home; his older brother Larry who lived with his wife and daughters in Toronto, Canada; his dad Lee, an electrician, and his mother, Viola Helen, a homemaker. Viola dropped out of college after the first semester to get married although she had hoped to become a home economics teacher.

My Husband Cliff's Mother Vi

Honey blonde-haired, blue-eyed Viola Helen Beaman was born a second-generation Koethe in Washington state. Her father Albert was a German immigrant. A stay-at-home mother of four, Vi Beaman spiced her life with the home arts. She ironed sheets and pressed shirts on a wide-angle ironer, a "thing," in the 1950s. She made appetizing cakes and pies, which were displayed with recipes on one of the local TV stations. (Her recipes for gumdrops, apple-orange brownies, maple praline cookies and cherry rolls remain in my files.) Like my own mother, Vi made dresses for her two daughters from feed bags. These were flour sacks printed with floral designs, a way to re-purpose a pantry staple into low-cost clothing. Later, she became astute at wheeling and dealing in real estate, flipping houses with Cliff's dad Lee to create another stream of income.

I finally met my husband's mother just days before our wedding. "Ooh, this is positively beautiful," she said as her hand caressed the satiny skirt of the wedding gown I had fashioned by hand.

1 – How We Met

I knew immediately she approved of me but cautioned, "You and Cliff may have quite a time adjusting to married life." She used the direct approach and didn't mince words about the huge difference obvious in our backgrounds: Her son was a Westerner used to city life, and I, his bride, a woman from the east coast with a rural Mennonite upbringing. I knew she cared about how we would fare, but I heard caution in her words.

For the wedding service, we had picked the hymn "In Christ there is no East or West," with lyrics that continue, "in Him no north or south, but one great fellowship of love throughout the whole wide earth." The words expressed my intention and hope, but as a starry-eyed bride, I had not lived them yet, nor had they been tested.

The elder Beamans, Lee and Vi, visited our home in Jacksonville, Florida, after our daughter Crista was born. Then we flew to Washington with two children, Crista and Joel, aged 1 ½ and 3. Grandma Beaman loved giving gifts to her grandchildren; she knitted pink and green caps and sweaters for Crista's dolls. For Joel, she bought a toy top with a merry-go-round motif, which he pumped up and down, up and down, gyrating with spins that wobbled until it toppled on its side.

We anticipated lots of inter-continental trips, back and forth from east to west. Even with the distance between us, we expected many family gatherings. But suddenly, Mother Beaman was struck with cancer and after a valiant fight, died in 1975 when she was only fifty-five years old. The heart of the family was gone.

My Checkered Life: A Marriage Memoir

Chapter 2

Tale of the Green Robe

I have a quilted green robe. It looks and feels like silk, but the fabric is probably rayon.

It has hung on a hook behind the bathroom door for a long, long time. And it has a history. My mother-in-law Viola gave me this robe as a Christmas gift before our children were born. It came from the Jantzen Company where she worked in Portland, Oregon, when American textiles were big business nationwide. In the 1930s, *Jantzen* was the seventh most recognized trademark.

Even doing imprecise math, you can tell that this is an old, old robe, but I still have it. I have held onto it for decades.

Why is that? First of all, it's in good shape, nearly floor-length and comfy warm when I dash from bedroom to kitchen on a cold January morning. "Will it ever wear out?" I wonder.

It's not in tatters. Still, I may have replaced it years ago simply because I've had it so long. It is old. But it came from a special person who no longer lives on this earth. There will be no more gifts from my mother-in-law, Vi Beaman. And so, I hang on to it.

Marian's green robe from Cliff's Mom Viola

These days my husband's Cliff's heritage lives on in Victorian-styled, framed pictures above our bedroom chest of drawers. His mother gazes with an expectant smile from one of the oval-shaped frames, her girlish face with deep-set blue eyes looking slightly left of the camera lens. In another photograph from the 1920s, his grandfather Albert Koethe stands stiffly by his bride, both locked in a formal pose not touching one another.

2 – Tale of the Green Robe

Albert forbade his children to speak German lest they become identified with the Hitler regime even as citizens in America. He believed the best way to survive in the new world was to hide his German heritage and assimilate American ways as soon as possible. Stern Albert ruled the household with strict decorum. Cliff tells me, "My mom said their house had to be spic and span, her dad insisting that the strings on the fringe of the carpet lie "just so" and getting angry if they looked askew.

Vi Beaman, teenager and baby picture

When Cliff visited Bethel Evangelical Methodist, a white clapboard church near Ridgefield, Washington, one of the older ladies approached him and, looking up at the tall man, uttered the name, "Al-bert, Al-bert" again and again, mesmerized by Cliff's striking resemblance to his grandfather. Fortunately for me, my husband, whose facial features reflect those of Albert Koethe, favors his father's side in personality, mostly even-tempered and less insistent on neatness and strict protocol.

His mother Vi seems a lot like my own mother Ruth, happy in the kitchen, baking cakes and pies, canning cherries and peaches in the summer, and preparing peas and beans from her garden for the freezer.

2 – Tale of the Green Robe

My Checkered Life: A Marriage Memoir

Chapter 3

Recipes: Viola Beaman and Ruth Longenecker

When our children were little and our family visited Mother and Daddy in Lancaster County, Pennsylvania, we could always count on an enamel-coated refrigerator drawer full of soup—either chicken corn soup or vegetable soup–to get us revived after a long car trip from Florida. Until the late 1990s, after an exhausting flight, we could open the fridge and find homemade soup in one of the drawers, ready to heat up.

Mother seldom used a recipe and when she did the proportions were often not included. No recipe? No problem for her.

Her vegetable soup recipe showed "potatoes" crossed out, but sometimes she added them.

After a couple of stabs at it, I coaxed Mom into being a little more precise about measurements for her savory vegetable soup.

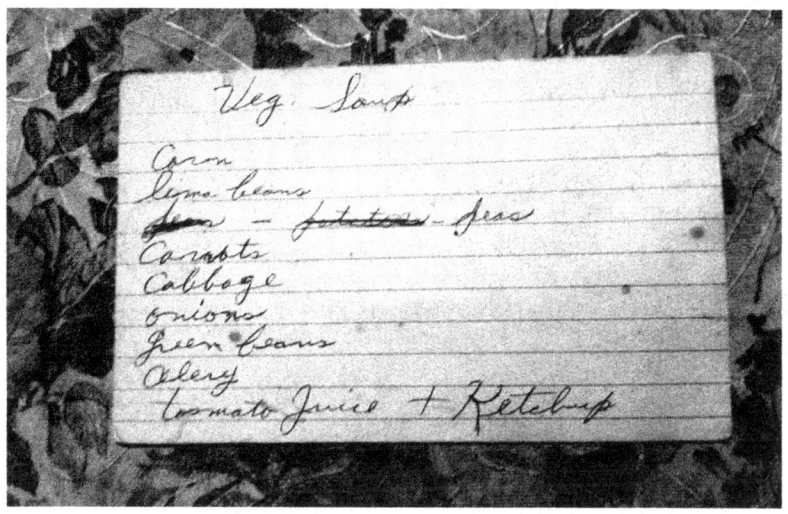

Handwritten recipe, vegetable soup

- Start with 2 1/2 pounds of chuck roast. Sear the meat and then bake it at 350 degrees until tender. It should be nice and brown and fall apart when you jab a fork into it! Save drippings.

- Cook separately: Carrots, celery and cabbage.
  Then add green beans, peas and corn.
  Be sure to keep the vegetable broth.

- Now add a quart of tomato juice (preferably canned from fresh tomatoes or tin canned crushed tomatoes.)

- 1/2 cup Heinz ketchup. Then combine beef, cut up, into vegetable + broth mixture and simmer.

The kitchen was Mother's "happy place." Well into her nineties, she'd make a big batch of vegetable soup when she knew her daughters and their families were gathering from Florida and eastern Pennsylvania.

3 – Recipes: Viola Beaman and Ruth Longnecker

Arriving at the homestead from the Harrisburg Airport in Middletown, we'd rush to open the refrigerator door, looking for a ceramic drawer down below, filled with her vegetable soup, a thick stew of colors and textures.

To furnish the soup, she kept a garden of tomatoes and beans. She harvested carrots, beans and tomatoes with a heart of gratitude. Plain, she never wanted to be fancy. She never quite understood my hankering for cosmetics, beauty that comes in jars. Yet I understood her love for canned fruits and vegetables, beauty in Mason jars that glowed like gems on wooden shelves in the cellar.

Mother Ruth Peeling Potatoes

Viola's Recipe

Cliff's Mother Vi too was a queen of culinary arts. She created tasty and delectable looking dishes in her kitchen at 2703 West Queen Avenue in Spokane, Washington. At one point, she attracted the attention of the local TV station, which photographed her dishes on a red and white checkered tablecloth in their studio.

3 – Recipes: Viola Beaman and Ruth Longnecker

Apple-Orange Brownies

INGREDIENTS

- 2/3 cup butter
- 2 tsp vanilla
- 1/2 tsp baking soda
- 1 cup applesauce
- 2 cups flour
- 1 cup chopped walnuts
- 2 cups brown sugar
- 2 tsp baking powder
- raisins or dates
- 2 eggs, beaten
- 2 tsp baking powder
- 1 tbsp grated orange rind
- 1/2 tsp salt

INSTRUCTIONS

1. In medium saucepan melt butter; remove from heat. Add 2 cups sugar, stir until blended. Cool.

2. Beat in applesauce, eggs, orange peel and vanilla. Sift flour, baking powder, salt and soda. Stir into applesauce mixture. Add nuts.

3. Spread in greased 15 ½ x 10 ½ x 1 inch baking pan. Bake in 350-degree oven for 25 to 30 minutes.

My Checkered Life: A Marriage Memoir

Chapter 4

Viola Beaman's Shoulder Bag and Bossler's Sewing Circle

About a year ago, I found several sheets of notebook paper on which Mother Viola had done intricate drawings of her handmade items: One a crocheted shoulder bag with intricate instructions on weaving the rows of yarn and border.

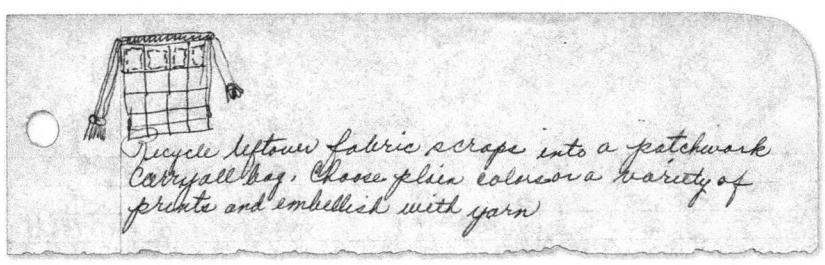

Patchwork Carryall Bag

Her notation in flowing ballpoint pen under the carryall bag: "Recycle leftover fabric scraps into a patchwork carryall bag. Choose plain colors or a variety of prints and embellish with yarn."

Crocheted Shoulder Bag

I was amazed at her detailed description of the fringe and shoulder strap, which required two people to make, each alternately twisting yarn around a dowel or pencil, handing yarn back and forth to one another. Vi was an artist with food and fabric and fine art, genes which her son, my husband, apparently inherited. His dad Lee had an artistic bent as well, doodling pencil designs as he talked on the phone mounted to the kitchen wall.

Bossler Mennonite Church was the hub of the Longenecker family's spiritual life and the school beside it, Washington School, the place where the Women's Sewing Circle fabricated comforters, baby clothing, blankets and quilts to meet the basic needs for clothing. Some of these gorgeous quilts are displayed here.

4 – Viola Beaman's Shoulder Bag and Bossler's Sewing Circle

Bossler Church quilt making

Even more than quilting I think Mother loved knitting comforters. For her, it was easier to see progress knotting a comforter than making a quilt. She liked the warm fluffy texture, and she could work on it by herself at home.

My Checkered Life: A Marriage Memoir

Chapter 5

Grandma Fannie Longenecker: Artifacts and Diary

Grandma Longenecker, my father's mother, was also a quilter. But clearing out Grandma's house the year Aunt Ruthie died in 2017, I discovered Grandma's art. Like my mother-in-law Viola's drawings, Grandma's was delicate and detailed.

Grandma Fannie Longenecker's Album of Postcards, 10 x 13 inches

Grandma died at age 89 and besides the diary, left behind other treasures, including artwork, I assume salvaged from her teenage years. When my sisters and I cleared out the house after Aunt Ruthie's death, we unearthed a magenta-toned album underneath a stack of other stuff in her bedroom closet. Although I knew Grandma dressed elegantly before she willingly adopted plain Mennonite garb, I never knew she had an artistic bent. She autographed her album in a decorative script and drew a picture of her own face, a genuine Victorian selfie! Who knew she experimented with sketching a self-portrait? The squarish-ness of what I remember as her adult long-hand is evident here, especially in the capital letters.

Fannie Martin's self-portrait

Victorian postcard artists kept a lid on romance, never straying too far into the sexy or salacious. In the scene shown here, the boastful driver with two armfuls of maidenhood seems to be oblivious to a recent car crash. His own? A stranger's?

5 – Grandma Fannie Longnecker: Artifacts and Diary

What's the real story here? I wonder.

The reverse side of this card gave no clue to the sender. However, Grandma thought the card was clever enough to keep.

Young Grandma: Postcard, Cad with Two Gals

Grandma's Diary

My thoughts:

Paging through the diaries of my Grandma Fannie Longenecker and my aunt Ruth Longenecker always evokes the past for me, usually in a good way. Diary entries help me look at my own life through the lens of my forebears. Just now, I catch a whiff of nostalgia when I "inhale" entries, one from Grandma Fannie

and others from Aunt Ruthie. In this way, they are joining the conversation, even here in these pages.

Secrets from Grandma Longenecker's Diary

I found just one leaf from a tablet my Grandma Longenecker began as a diary, below. She may have intended to add more. Or maybe she wrote more, and I haven't yet discovered those pages.

5 – Grandma Fannie Longnecker: Artifacts and Diary

Wed. Apr 1, 1931

Today is a day, long to be remembered, it blew and rained all night. The chickens were stolen out of the chicken house, and hens and two roosters were in the barn. And that's what was left. Also, all of Ray's rabbits are gone. Two state troopers were here to investigate.

After recovering from this shock, H. R. [my Grandpa Henry] accompanied E. F. Groff [Elmer Groff, a neighbor] and his wife Anna to Elizabethtown and this property was transferred to us. To soothe our sorrow, [Anna Groff and I] made Easter eggs, our success was fine. In the evening Clayton Nolt was here from Bird-in-Hand, and on top of all our luck (hard and otherwise) sold H. R. and Son 12 Cloverhill Brand Rabbits. I am quilting Ruthie [my aunt, her daughter] a little pink quilt.

Thurs. Apr. 2, 1931

Ironed and mended this a.m. also quilted a little, after dinner H. R. and I plant 6 cherry trees, 3 sour & 3 black. Norman Rutt gave us the trees, Hope this one and many generations can enjoy them.

My thoughts

Before I was ten years old, I remember my dad, Ray, repeating in disbelief: "Chickens, chickens, why would they steal chickens?" as he paced the kitchen floor, retelling the story. Now as I recall the incident through the long lens of time, I have concluded that because robbery of any kind was rare in rural Lancaster County in those days, when it happened, it created an uproar. The Big Guns were called in. In this century, school shootings and kidnappings make the news, not petty theft as described here. I have noticed too that Grandma Longenecker refers to Grandpa as "H. R.," who died when I was five. I wonder now if such a formal reference reflected her esteem of him, or revealed the age difference, her husband fifteen years her senior. Even then, her writing reveals she found solace in making something beautiful, a little pink quilt, likely checkered with squares of pastel fabric remnants.

I knew Grandma Longenecker was "fancy" before she became plain in dress, which I describe in my memoir, *Mennonite Daughter:*

> *Grandma was Fannie Horst Martin Longenecker, a handsome woman from Middletown, Pennsylvania, who was fancy (modern) in Victorian-era fashion before she married her plain Mennonite husband, Henry Risser Longenecker, who owned the farm-implement shop in Rheems. Pennsylvania. Before she married, she wore an otter hat and a fur-trimmed coat, fancy "costumes" we children saw hanging on black iron hooks along the wall of her attic stairs.*

> *When we were older and married, Aunt Ruthie surprised each of her nieces, Janice, Jean, and me, with a white-and-gold box. Each contained a ring from Grandma:*

5 – Grandma Fannie Longnecker: Artifacts and Diary

One amethyst, another amethyst and pearl, and, best of all, her opal engagement ring. Mine was amethyst and pearl. Lucky Janice got the opal and Jean the larger amethyst. Where had Grandma hidden those gorgeous pieces of jewelry all those years? When we cleared out the house after Aunt Ruthie's death in 2017, more treasures from Grandma emerged: an ornate buckle, jeweled hat pins, and his-and-her wedding rings of pure gold.

Grandma, who wore elegance in her youth, seemed so contented wearing Mennonite garb later on. Their wedding photograph shows her and Henry, wearing traditional wedding outfits, she with a decorative jacket over a belted white dress, he with a regular suit and tie. Grandma adopted wearing plain apparel when they joined the Mennonite church after their marriage, the custom in those days. From then on, she wore a plain dress with a cape every day under her apron.

(from Chapter 11, *Mennonite Daughter: The Story of a Plain Girl*, "Grandma's Early Fancy Days")

Although my Grandma never seemed to regret leaving the "fancy" for the plain, she continued working the soil in her garden, planting strawberries, green beans, or flowers, which exploded in floral fantasy from spring's sun-yellow crocuses to autumn's saffron zinnias and amethyst chrysanthemums. All her life, she created pretty things with her hands. She exuded joy in gardening and stitching patches for quilts on her sewing machine.

I detect the same impulse in myself, my heart leaping up when a blog post forms from the flash of an idea, or when something beautiful in nature smacks me over the head, inspiring me to create a haiku:

Each hibiscus bloom

Like manna, just one each day

Nourishing my soul

Hisbiscus from my patio garden

5 – Grandma Fannie Longnecker: Artifacts and Diary

My Checkered Life: A Marriage Memoir

Chapter 6

Aunt Ruth Longenecker: Autograph Book and Diaries

My Aunt Ruthie Longenecker kept diaries too, one recording five of her teenage years and five others, where she kept accounts of her work at home, her volunteer work for Bossler Mennonite Church and for my dad's business along with reflections about her professional life as teacher and school principal.

An autograph book from her senior year at Elizabethtown (Pennsylvania) High School is a keepsake which reflects the spirit of youth in the 1930s.

I found Aunt Ruthie's autograph book from 1935 at the bottom of this painted chest under a pile of blankets, dolls, and vintage clothing.

Her classmates from Elizabethtown High School class of 1935 wrote in her autograph book. Some sayings were sweet, some were silly. Three were translatable from Latin and German. I also discovered Ruthie's math teacher, Miss Dulebohn, who taught me algebra as well.

Aunt Ruthie's chest and Autograph Book

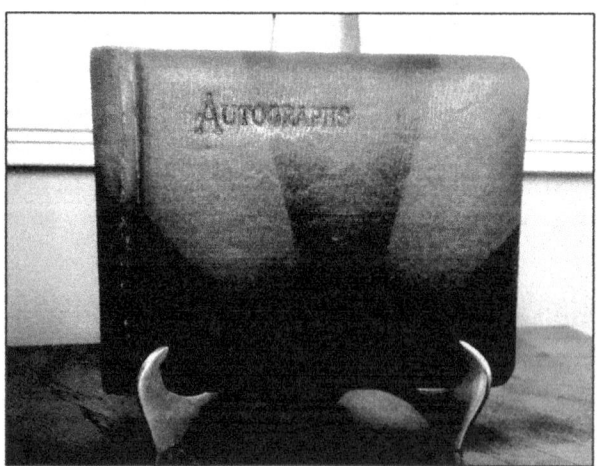

6 – Aunt Ruth Longenecker: Autograph Book and Diaries

The signatures on more than seventy pink, blue and beige pages featured classmates with Pennsylvania Dutch origins: Blottenberger, Ebersole, Hertzler, Raffensperger, Schlosser, Ulrich, and Wolgemuth. But I found a student named Madeira and a Stephens to add the flavor of Hispanic and British family origins. Seen through the gauze of nostalgia, these entries seem sentimental or silly, some even corny. The teachers contributed serious ones.

> *May you always be friends with Dame Fortune, may you never meet [her] daughter Miss Fortune.*
> – Nancy Garber

> *It's hard to lose the boy you love / When your heart is full of hope / but it's harder still to find a towel / When your eyes are full of soap.*
> – "Stet"

> *Here's till you slide down the banister of love / Into the ash can of matrimony.*
> – "Millie"

> *You'll go far on your way to success / Whether or not you wear a cute dress / Always be happy, and always be gay / Remember tomorrow is not far away.*
> – Anna (Claudia)

Teacher Signatures

"Were die Leiter hinauf will, muss bei der untersten sprosse anfaugen."
Signed, *Dein deutscher lehrer,*
– T. H. Ebersole

[Translation of text from German teacher: "If you want to climb the ladder, you have to start at the bottom rung."]

Always have a star farther than your grasp as your goal.
– Mr. Bishop

Who walks the world with soul awake / Finds beauty everywhere.
– May Dulebohn, who quoted Florence Earle Coates in *"Friends Intelligencer"*

These admonitions from Aunt Ruthie's autograph book, peculiar to the times include one from Miss Dulebohn, algebra teacher. With her Eleanor Roosevelt-esque hair style, she inspired fear and respect as she strode with sure, steady steps up and down aisles of student desks, extolling the marvels of advanced math. Miss Dulebohn was my math teacher too but much later in her career. I wonder whether she wore her hair the same way when my aunt was her student. Miss Dulebohn, stern and severely disciplined, never appeared to me to be a

6 – Aunt Ruth Longenecker: Autograph Book and Diaries

Aunt Ruthie Longenecker's Diaries

fashion-plate. Perhaps she had a soft side, which she concealed from her students. Her quote chosen for Ruthie's autograph book may suggest that.

As an adult my aunt was not a quilter, but she knitted sweaters for herself, and for my sisters Janice, Jean, and me. Although she made her own dresses on her Pfaff sewing machine, she also knitted together words in her diaries, trying to make sense of the patchwork of her days. Like her, my stories reveal the checkered pattern of my own life, a tapestry with loose threads and tangled knots underneath, but the emerging design sometimes revealing new patterns, showing a pathway forward.

My Checkered Life: A Marriage Memoir

Quilting with Words

Aunt Ruth Longenecker, my father's sister, whom we usually called "Ruthie," helped develop my love of learning, gave me my first piano lessons, took me on the train to the Philadelphia Zoo, to my first theatre performance, and recorded many of our family's antics on a 16-millimeter movie camera. She was also adept at shooting starlings, crows, or groundhogs that messed with her garden plantings. Yet she never showed me how to aim and pull the trigger on her 22-gauge rifle, kept stored in her kitchen closet, maybe because she thought controlling the starling population was her personal purview.

Aunt Ruthie had a heart-shaped hairline and hazel eyes. Two thin lines formed lips that did not suggest any laxness. As sharp and as versatile as a Swiss army knife, she sported a watch with a crocodile-skin strap around her wrist. Like my mother, she wanted to keep track of time. Yet her bedroom dresser revealed her softer side — perfume and powder puff, gifts from her teacher friends. And on the bedroom wall hung evidence of her hobby: a signed 1980s oil painting of daffodils and violets, a spring vision in yellow and lavender.

Aunt Ruth chose the single life, or maybe it chose her. She never married, and the few men she did date didn't measure up to her standards. She dismissed a potential

6 – Aunt Ruth Longenecker: Autograph Book and Diaries

beau by saying to my grandmother, "He's careless." Instead, from the crown of her head to the soles of her tie-up shoes, my aunt became a work wizard. Whoever wrote the blurb for her 1935 yearbook acknowledged her brilliance in English and math and predicted that she would be a "thorough and patient" teacher. However, patient did not describe her attitude toward getting the job done. Along with teaching, she plowed into keeping tax records for the West Donegal Township, stitched up seams for her handmade dresses, kept the books for the church and for my dad's shop, worked in the family fields during the summer, and mowed the lawn in the early years with a push mower on the two-and-a-half-acre property she shared with Grandma. "She became a valuable help to Mother, who didn't drive, taught her how to sew, how to clean, and make a big company dinner for twelve or more," Grandma said of her daughter in my sister's sociology notes.

(from Chapter 6, *Mennonite Daughter: The Story of a Plain Girl*, "My Two Mothers")

Inside a painted chest in her bedroom. I discovered Aunt Ruthie Longenecker's diaries after her death in 2017. As a youngster, I have an image of her walking around the house with a yellow Dixon-Ticonderoga pencil slotted at an angle between her ear and hair. It's often baffling and sometimes infuriating that she wrote mostly in pencil, a wood-encased core of graphite and clay. But with magnification, her cursive penmanship is readable.

The two entries from 1945 juxtapose ordinary life in her household with the detonation of a bomb over Hiroshima, patches of life-as-usual with dark blots of the unthinkable.

> **August 6, 1945**
> *Rainy Monday, so we decided since we had all yesterday's dishes to wash, we'd clean the cupboards. We cleaned the desk and the red [cherry] cupboard, washed all the dishes, etc. Uncle Joe stopped in for dinner. Today an atomic bomb was released over Japan. It is very destructive – weighing 11 pounds, it is equivalent to 300 carloads of T.N.T.*

> **August 7, 1945**
> *Sun in & sun out, so we washed – it dried [on the clothesline] & is ironed. This afternoon we had 3 showers – one a thunderstorm. Now it seems quite clear. Ray brought [my sister] Janice down in the scooter [equipped with a rear bin] today. She's only 10 months old.*

That atomic bomb surely had been destructive although no one knew to what extent. It was never tested for there was no spot possible in the U. S.

Washing, ironing, cooking, and cleaning amidst news of a BOMB exploding in a foreign land, killing hundreds of thousands of people, likely announced first on the radio, and the next day, in the newspaper.

6 – Aunt Ruth Longenecker: Autograph Book and Diaries

Aunt Ruthie's diary entry reflects the sentiment which W. H. Auden expresses in *"Musee des Beaux Arts,"* a poem he wrote just before the beginning of World War II in 1938. Like Auden, my aunt's diary probably demonstrates that while cataclysmic events occur, the rest of the world continues on in a mundane way. Life goes on in spite of tragedy, the poet implies.

In my own life, I've witnessed the assassination of President John F. Kennedy in 1963, his brother Bobby a few years later, and then Dr. Martin Luther King. In 1986 came the fateful explosion of the rocket in the Challenger mission, and in 2001 the horrific attack on the Twin Towers in New York City.

Yet, as these events occurred, I have pushed ahead, beginning a teaching career at Lancaster Mennonite School, getting married to my life partner Cliff, experiencing pregnancy with our first child, daughter Crista, the year when astronauts walked on the moon, and recoiling at the unimaginable images of planes hitting the Twin Towers in 2001 in the midst of my teaching at Florida State College in Jacksonville, Florida. Indeed, life goes on in spite of outrageous tragedy, and we somehow persevere through it all.

Just like clockwork, classes began right after Labor Day at Rheems Elementary School in Pennsylvania. Aunt Ruthie was my teacher in the first four grades. She taught grades 1-4 simultaneously in a two-room school, where eight grades (each with a teacher) assembled under one roof with a bell. The rooftop bell punctuated high points of the school day: the beginning of classes and the ending of recess. Excerpts from Aunt Ruthie's diary give a glimpse into two opening days of school several years before I was old enough to be her student.

> **September 5, 1944**
> *Surprise! Out to school and opened the door and what? Mr. Greiner had Kem-Toned the ceiling and walls with light green & done the woodwork in white. Don't say that didn't lighten things up. Carl Floyd, 1st grader, surely is sweet. He's the only first grader who had to cry a little, probably because he'd left the familiarity of home and felt scared and upset in a new environment.*

6 – Aunt Ruth Longenecker: Autograph Book and Diaries

Note: In 1941 the Sherwin-Williams Company introduced Kem-Tone Wall Finish, the first commercially successful, durable, interior wall paint.

> **September 4, 1945**
> *Well, today school started. 29 on roll, 2 graciously given from Grandview, the kind anyone is anxious to hand over. But they're a nice bunch — lights in school, cellar cleared, and new reading books. And as usual tearing my hind leg off trying to get around. Worked at Bldg. tonight.*

My thoughts

It appears that Miss Longenecker may have been given two extra students from another school for some reason. Nevertheless, she apparently is going to make the best of it, although she implies her low expectations for them. In those days, teachers had duties far beyond teaching, making sure the "physical plant" was up to snuff, a job now usually reserved for maintenance staff. The school cellar was a site for our Halloween fun house for grades 1-8.

Much like Marty McFly in "Back to the Future," I was thrown back to the mid-1940s, though in a Terraplane Hudson, not a deluxe DeLorean. The diary entry below thrust me back to the time I was pre-school age.

I remember riding to Cherry Hill School near Milton Grove, Pa. with my aunt in her Hudson, now obsolete. I stared out the oval windows in the back seat. It was the only version of kindergarten available to a five-year-old girl in rural Pennsylvania during that era. My mother must have been happy to send me off. She had her hands full with me and my sisters at home when Jean was an infant and Janice a toddler. And when the school year ended, the whole class celebrated with homemade ice cream from a wooden churn!

And then an entry from three years later, where I appear as a singing partner and classroom helper:

> **May 18, 1944**
> *Praise the fishes! No. 180 done. And no strings. Had Marian along. We sang, reviewed & put books away. Then Joe G's [Greiner] graciously contributed 8 gallons of Ice Cream and our 4 gallons gave plenty. We also had chips, pretzel sticks, cookies & drinks. Mummas [our neighbors] have the measles.*

Schools in the twenty-first century are larger than two rooms with students, grades 1-8. Typically, students are separated into grades and sections. Teachers these days are plagued by academic benchmarks they must reach, set by a distant school board. Thus, teachers are often tempted to "teach to the test," so the district can recognize their classroom's achievement, contributing to high marks as an "A-grade" school.

This brush of nostalgia perhaps paints over the pain of teachers with rulers ready to smack the hands of students who don't catch on to math reading problems, which I recall happening in my classroom. What makes me smile now, though, are the good times, like singing every morning before pulling out our textbooks. Above the keys on my piano in our home is a songbook titled The Golden Book of Favorite Songs.

At Rheems School, we had our daily ritual: Bell ringing from the school-house steeple (always by a boy), Bible reading, the Lord's Prayer, the Pledge of Allegiance, and then singing from this songbook before lessons began.

This is My Father's World, My Country 'Tis of Thee, and Home on the Range were staples in our little ochre-toned songbook. But many of the lyrics we sang would be considered insulting and even offensive to various ethnic and racial groups in this era. For example, Old Solomon Levi, playing to the stereotype of the wily Jewish merchant:

> *My name is Solomon Levi*
> *At my store in Salem Street,*
> *There's where you find your coats and vests,*
> *And ev'rything else that's neat:*
> *I've second-handed Ulsterettes,*
> *And ev'rything else that's fine;*
> *For all the boys—they trade with me,*
> *At one hundred and forty-nine.*
> *Chorus.*
> *Oh, Mister Levi, Levi, tra, la, la, la.*
> *Poor Solomon Levi, tra la, la, la, la, la, la, la*

Next, we might sing My Old Kentucky Home with what was back then dubbed the Negro dialect. "The sun shines bright in my Old Kentucky Home, Tis summer, the darkies are gay."

What?! "Darkies are gay...?" Innocent of the dissonance in the words we would discover offensive later, we sang the chorus at the top of our lungs. "Weep no more, my lady. Oh, weep no more to-day: / We will sing one song for the old Kentucky home / for the Old Kentucky home, Far away."

The dialect continued when we belted out Dixie: "I wish I was in de land ob cotton, Old times dar am not forgotten, Look a-way! Look a-way! Look a-way Dixie Land." There was even a winking nod to obesity in some stanzas: "Dar's buckwheat cakes, an' Injun batter, " makes you fat or a little fatter . . . .

And finally, the songbook contained the wistful, "When You and I Were Young, Maggie," and "My Grandfather's Clock" sung by youngsters who had no conception of aging or of mortality.

6 – Aunt Ruth Longenecker: Autograph Book and Diaries

My Checkered Life: A Marriage Memoir

Chapter 7

Cliff's Early School Days And Marian's Preschool

My husband Cliff admits he has sketchy memories of his early school days. Looking back, he does remember reciting the Pledge of Allegiance but certainly not Bible reading or singing from a Golden Book of Favorite Songs with piano accompaniment.

"I was a dud," he says of his performance as a student. "In kindergarten at Field Elementary School in Spokane, Washington, I liked playtime, lunch, and nap time lying on a mat." He also admits to two short-lived love affairs. One with Nancy, which ended when she went down a slide and the romance fell apart. In fourth grade, he was late for school one day, and Mitzi, a girl who might have been French, ran by and kissed him on the cheek. That too was the end of the romance, just a few seconds long.

1969 Hammered Copper Bird

Cliff continues, "My sixth-grade teacher, Mr. Carpenter, believed in corporal punishment. After three warnings, I refused to stop talking. He had me march to the front of the classroom, bend over while he spanked me with a heavy-duty wooden paddle. I was humiliated. The spanking hurt and I never needed that chastisement again."

7 – Cliff's Early School Days and Marian's Preschool

My interest in school piqued a little in sixth grade. I looked forward to two days each of music and art classes. My art teacher, robust, and muscular, could catch Garr fish with bare hands. In his art class I could shine. One of my classmates, Eugene Papier, was my competition. "I thought he could draw better than I could, and I tried to emulate him."

During Cliff's high school years, his family moved to Idaho, where he attended Idaho Falls High School. He had the privilege of taking art classes with the renowned Helen Hoff Aupperle, noted for her painting of indigenous Indians and pastel landscapes. Not until much later, did he realize how famous she had become.

Over the years, his mom recognized his talent in art and complimented his drawings. She grew up with Strauss waltzes and bought him an accordion probably because she wanted him to value the music she grew up with. She sacrificed getting a new couch to replace the old one with "sprung" cushions, so he could take accordion lessons. But there was a caveat. When guests came to visit, he had to show his art work to them, and he was also required to play waltzes.

"Will you get out your accordion and play for the Hege's?" his Mom would ask. Once he said, "No" and his mom looked shocked, but then turned stern, "Do you want to play for them or not have supper?"

I played the "Under the Double Eagle" march," because I didn't want to miss out on her delicious pan-fried chicken, he admits.

Aunt Ruthie's Diary and My Birthday

Marian in highchair enjoying her cake

I don't remember my first birthday. Can anyone recall that far back in time? But early images come to mind as I reminisce: The red and silver oilcloth on the kitchen table that I viewed from the wooden highchair with pink, blue, and green lines

7 – Cliff's Early School Days and Marian's Preschool

tracing the oval contours on the back. All four of us children sat in it. And I remember the backyard at my parents' house, the clothesline, and of course the outhouse, in later years half-hidden by a mulberry bush. Novelist Vladimir Nabokov notes that these flashes of memory begin marking the time we become sentient beings, when we become aware of who we are.

Where my memory fails, Aunt Ruthie's diary fills in some detail of those early days and years, July 21-24, 1944.

July 2, 1944
Friday, Cloudy, cleaned, trimmed <u>some</u> yard. In corn field & pulled weeds this P.M. A Promise of plenty of work for tomorrow. Marian can say all of "Humpty Dumpty" and most of all other rhymes. She insisted on having a big paper clamp on each pigtail.

July 22, 1944
I say, What is the use of cleaning? Who'd ever know I scrubbed both porches, Washed up & waxed the kitchen and bathroom, washed all the windows. The dog tracked up the porch. The ducks messed up the walks, someone spilt ground [dirt] on the steps, etc.

July 23, 1944
Sunday – HOT! Down to see Aunt Ellen & Anna this eve. Played croquet with Ben & Mary Emenheiser, Anna & I. Today was Ruth's [her sister-in-law and my mother's] birthday.

My Checkered Life: A Marriage Memoir

July 24, 1944
Marian's birthday and quite a day for her. As for me – not so wonderful. At 6 I tied Baa [her sheep] around & he was nice as could be. At 9:30 came home from Ray's & there he lay – He must have eaten nightshade or something. I'm done!!!

My thoughts:

I was three at the time her sheep died, and I may be older than three in the photo below. Obviously, Aunt Ruthie was devastated at the death of her pet. I wonder if she bought another lamb. If so, I may not have noticed much difference, especially if she kept the name "Baa." She had the custom of naming her new pets as though they were an incarnation of the former one. In fact, over a period of decades, she had a series of four Schnauzers, all named Fritzie, and dubbed with Roman numerals I, II, III, IV.

Pet sheep Baa

7 – Cliff's Early School Days and Marian's Preschool

I have a photo of Cliff, possibly at two years old. I can't tell precisely because the picture is not dated. But my tow-headed husband-to-be is wearing a smudged face, dirty bib-overalls and playing with an upside-down dump truck.

Cliff at age two

When we looked at this photograph together, he chuckled, "If you knew me then, you probably wouldn't have liked to have me as a playmate because I got dirty and liked monkeying around with tools, and you liked to play with dolls in your doll-house, everything in apple pie order."

And then comes a record of my fourth birthday a year later in 1945.

Intentionally or not, imitating the style of *British diarist Samuel Pepys*, Aunt Ruthie records the weather and mundane activities but sneaks in clues to her work ethic, her social life, and historic detail about extreme weather. She was a 27-year-old unmarried school teacher in the mid-1940s.

July 21, 1945
Beans, beans, & weeds I pulled this A.M. & some this afternoon. – At 3:30 Myra, Ethel, Anna & I left for Doylestown. We're visiting Esther, Anna, Maggie and Emma Hiestand. Did I ever see some beautiful evergreen trees. This has been a beautiful day

July 22, 1945
We were at Doylestown [Mennonite] church. These girls surely are friendly. At 3:30 we left for home in some rain. But we never realized what we were coming to. At Lancaster Bridge the water was over the road about 2 ft & at Mt. Joy 4 feet, so over water & finally drive around by East Petersburg. Elizabethtown really was flooded. There was much damage, Clearview Diner [a mobile restaurant] was moved across the road.

July 23, 1945
Mon. cloudy this A.M. Had cleared some by P.M. Working away on bookkeeping & that says all.

7 – Cliff's Early School Days and Marian's Preschool

July 24, 1945
Tues. cloudy but cleared some. Ma washed & I ironed most everything tonight. Received an invitation to [Phares] Jr. Longenecker's shower on Aug. 4 & today Marian was four. I got her a sweat shirt & she insisted on wearing it in all this heat.

In retrospect, I have no clear memory of what this sweatshirt looked like on my birthday in 1945, but my aunt was present in my life as a second mother even then. Grandma Longenecker had only two children, my father and Aunt Ruthie. At the time I was my aunt's oldest niece. Clearly, she doted on me, a child she may have even then seen as someone she could mold like clay into a model little maid.

My aunt's diary used the word "insisted" referring to my strong will. I found it again in another entry, which makes me conclude that personality traits that surface in early years often remain into adulthood, maybe even in a magnified form. I recognize this trait now on my best days as persistence and resolve.

My Checkered Life: A Marriage Memoir

Chapter 8

My Two Mothers

I had two mothers. And they were almost the same person. Almost. My mother and my aunt had the same name, Ruth M. Longenecker. Even the middle initial was the same, Mother's "M" for "Metzler" and Aunt Ruthie's "M" for "Martin." Concerned that their files might get mixed up, they were careful never to choose the same doctor, lawyer, or bank. From their names, you may assume they were practically interchangeable. In fact, when my aunt was admitted to a nursing home in the early stages of dementia at age ninety-three, she said to my mother, "You could sit here, and I could go home. We have the same names. No one would notice!" However, apart from their vital statistics, German-Swiss family ancestry, and geographical proximity, my mother Ruth and my Aunt Ruth were worlds apart in personal choices and life paths.

My mother Ruth was a farm girl, born and bred. Her dream for life, she mentioned more than once, was to be a good farm wife

My Checkered Life: A Marriage Memoir

and mother to four or more. Her pride in being a wife expressed itself in a large, framed wedding photo on top of the piano. My black-bow-tied dad then wore the same pleased expression I noticed when he bagged deer. My mother's attire was a crepe, V-necked cape dress with sleeves snug from wrist to elbow, where it puffed out and then calmed down at the shoulder. Tiny buttons covered in the same fabric lined the snug part. I am sure she made the dress herself.

A mistress of the culinary arts, Mom loved to entertain, thrilled to add leaves to her dining-room table for a dozen or more. Two sets of fine crystal stood in her corner china closet, one with etched-in lines near the lip, the other floral. The goblets and sherbets, along with ivory china with a silver scalloped edging, decorated the feast when Mother invited company. Five or six times a year, she sat at one end of the dining table close to the kitchen so she could serve a formal dinner. Always on Sunday. Usually after church. As a hostess, she wanted everything perfect. Once when I was helping, her fist flew to her mouth when she opened the oven to find the roast already done and the gravy bubbling like crazy on the stove. She probably wanted to swear (she never used curse words), but I sped up to keep the courses moving along, taking her agonized gesture as a scream for help.

(from Chapter 6, *Mennonite Daughter: The Story of a Plain Girl*, "My Two Mothers")

8 – My Two Mothers

Strife between the Women

I realized growing up that I benefited from an extended family, including strong feminine role models: Grandma Longenecker, Aunt Ruthie Longenecker, and Mother Ruth. Such favor comes often with conditions though. It surely did in my case. My mother, who completed school up to eighth grade, took pleasure in dressing her three little daughters in outfits she embellished with embroidery when we were small. She reveled in making bountiful meals and worked hard in the tomato field and in her garden. Aunt Ruthie, on the other hand, had a college education, a profession, and knew how to drive long before Mother got her own license.

My sisters and I could observe first-hand the pros and cons in choosing two different life paths for women in the 1950s and 60s. However, we also noticed the tug-of-war between aunt and mother, both vying for the upper-hand in our upbringing. I believe our mother saw that her sister-in-law had an "edge," able to give us piano lessons and take us to the zoo in her Studebaker. Aunt Ruthie, never to be our biological mother, nevertheless tried to imprint us with her image of fulfilling womanhood, which I could sense rankled my mother. Thus, the push and pull between the two women. Once they called a truce temporarily when my father was suddenly stricken with lymphoma, "I'm with you all the way," Aunt Ruthie said to Mother, who solemnly repeated these words to me a few months before Daddy died. I savored the remark coming at a time when our family so desperately needed to pull together.

My Checkered Life: A Marriage Memoir

Chapter 9

Mother and Daughter Define Beauty

When my Mother and Daddy were dating, my mom told me her then-boyfriend Ray smiled at her, "You are the prettiest thing I ever saw!" It was true. Their wedding photo shows a bride with thick, raven hair and a curvy figure. Even past middle-age, she had clear, unwrinkled skin and dimples. In her coffin at age 96, there were dark-brown strands of hair among the silver.

As a farm wife, she wore brimmed bonnets to keep the sun out of her face when she worked in the garden and picked tomatoes in our nine-acre field in Bainbridge, Pennsylvania, but I don't think she ever wore sunscreen or thought of smearing foundation on her face. Lipstick and mascara were certainly out of the question.

Beauty in Jars

One morning we had a conversation about our different definitions of beauty when Mom assessed my cosmetics on her bathroom vanity: "What are you doing with all that stuff?" She didn't wait for an answer. "I wouldn't know what to do with it all," she added as she eyed my jars of moisturizer, foundation, concealer, makeup remover.

Mom continued, "I'm happy with the face God gave me. If He had wanted it different, He would have made me different." Now elderly, she recalled again the compliment her husband paid her when they were dating: "You're the prettiest thing I ever saw!" Even Shakespeare's Hamlet would side with Mother as he chides, "God has given you one face, and you make yourself another."

9 – Mother and Daughter Define Beauty

Beauty in Jars, Another View

Mother had a smooth complexion for her age—genes or good eating, probably a combination of both. A lover of food, she sometimes asked after eating a breakfast of her Honey Nut Cheerios, juice, banana, and coffee, "Do we need a piece of chocolate now?" as she turned to open a box of NaNa's Homemade Sweet Treats.

Our last chore together that Pennsylvania visit in 2013 was to wash the jars for canning in her basement cellar. Except for a few vintage jars, she was giving most of them away as she neared 95. "I'm done with canning," she said. Filled with tomato juice, beets, peaches, apricots, pickled cantaloupe, strawberry jam, and pickles, the jars formed a beautiful collage lining her wooden shelves, glistening with a diamond sparkle from the single bulb light hanging from the ceiling.

Before Mom had a freezer, green beans added yet another hue. Every year, her mother-in-law Fannie helped her chop fresh vegetables for piccalilli, or what the Pennsylvania Dutch call chow-chow. Now she was donating most of the jars to Goodwill, but keeping some vintage Ball and Mason Jars. A few had old fashioned metal clasps that hugged the glass lids. "These are very valuable," she told me.

All the cliches come to mind as I reminisce: *Beauty is where you find it. Beauty is in the eye of the beholder. You're beautiful inside and out.*

I say, "Beauty is ageless."

To Reflect

What memories of canning, long ago or recent, do you have?

How do you define beauty?

Share your story with a friend or relative.

9 – Mother and Daughter Define Beauty

My Checkered Life: A Marriage Memoir

Chapter 10

Beamans and Longeneckers Socialize with Relatives

*H*ordes of Metzlers, Martins, and Longeneckers peopled the happy scenes of my early life. As the seasons rolled along, relatives gathered for Easter, Thanksgiving, and Christmas with summertime picnics in farm meadows and Lititz Springs Park. While we often saw my Grandma Longenecker and Aunt Ruthie who lived close by, aunts and uncles from my mother's Metzler side often visited Sunday afternoons.

We squealed when we heard the wheels of their cars crush the gravel on the driveway at Anchor Road, "Oh, Clydes's are here!" Or, here come the Brenemans (or, Abe's, Landis's, or Leroy's)! Except for holidays, no one called ahead, announcing a visit. They just appeared at our house. We loved when our cousins tumbled out of their cars, knowing we were in for an afternoon playing with dolls with lidded eyes or competing in board games like Uncle Wiggly. Late afternoon, before the dairy farmers had to head home to milk cows, we treated them to Breyer's Neapolitan ice cream, Utz's pretzels, or Charley's Chips. Naturally, they returned the favor when we dropped by.

My husband's family was more isolated in Spokane, Washington, tucked away in the northeast corner of Washington State close to the Canadian border. The Beamans lived far from close relatives situated in the southern part of the state near Camas. When Cliff was in kindergarten, his family moved to a drier part of the state to accommodate his health. The moist atmosphere of Camas, along with the sulphuric smell of paper mills, triggered Cliff's asthma attacks. He felt as though he was suffocating. To alleviate some of his symptoms, a doctor prescribed an orange pill sub-lingually, which produced a high-pitched voice and made him giggle. When symptoms were severe, he sometimes ended up in bed under a tent filled with menthol vapors. He usually had to sleep upright and most definitely stay far, far away from feather pillows, dust and mold. In Spokane, where his dad found work as an electrician, Cliff could breathe more easily. However, isolation from close relatives was the price his family had to pay to ensure a healthy son.

Cliff's Turn: Winter in Spokane

Delights mixed with some disappointments describe holidays when I was growing up in Spokane, Washington, from kindergarten through eighth grade. The Arctic cold and moisture from the Cascades produced huge mounds of fresh white snow in the winter. In December my older brother Larry and two younger sisters Joyce and Kathy had a hilarious time,

10 – Beamans and Longneckers Socialize with Relatives

enjoying "snow" days off from school, especially around the Christmas holidays.

After a snowfall, my brother Larry and I layered several shirts and sweaters beneath a heavy winter coat, crawled into our blue jeans, pulled on thick gloves and earmuffs and a woolen stocking cap. When we stepped out from the warm, comfy house, cold air slapped our faces.

On West Queen Avenue where our family lived, a dozen houses looped around its East and West block. My brother Larry and I pulled our sleds with stiff lengths of rope over the fresh blanket of snow leaving a thin trail behind. We sucked in freezing air, bellowing out vaporous rings of breath.

Although our own street was quite flat, the adjoining streets to our west angled downward. *What a thrill to whiz by so many houses, our sled-speed accelerating by the block!* The ride was exhilarating going down, but a hard twenty-five-minute exhausting climb back up. After several runs, we were physically spent, trudging home stiffly with wet-soaked pants which had quickly turned into puppet-like frozen legs. My parents couldn't afford the soft winter snow pants that some lucky kids wore.

We often started sledding in the late afternoon but the winter light faded quickly. It was dark when we returned, making the soft yellow street lights appear alien and spooky. Stepping up four icy steps and bursting through the heavy front door at home, Mom commanded us, "Take off your stiff clothing and get into a bathtub of lukewarm water." Anything hotter would sting our almost frozen limbs. After finishing our bath, we enjoyed hot chocolate and a snack. Sometimes if we came back extremely late, Mom warmed some milk in a pan, poured it over some pieces of bread, and to bed we would go, instantly falling asleep.

Before Christmas Dad bought an evergreen tree and nailed a few pieces of board in the form of a plus sign to the trunk of the tree. Our decorations were homemade. Sometimes we popped popcorn in an iron basket over the flickering flames in the fireplace and with sticky fingers, strung them one by one to make a several foot-long decoration, which we would wind around the tree. We also added a few glass decorations, strings of colored glass lights (which became hot to the touch) and draped silvery tinsel onto every bough. We topped the tree with a star made with tinfoil. The tree had no reservoir with water, so the hot Christmas lights placed close to the fireplace could have caught fire. By New Year's Day, the tree itself became so dry it could have burst into flames. It was a miracle it never did.

Presents became a sore spot for me in my teenage years. When I was younger, I remember my excitement getting toy trucks, cranes, footballs, and Erector sets. On two holidays, I remember getting an electric train set which actually had smoke coming out of the engine. A year later I got extra cars for the set and track segments to allow the train to make lots of turns. Best of all, I could goose the dial on the transformer on the longer straight lengths. The Erector sets were a great way to be creative. My brother and I would usually get a softball and glove from my Grandmother Gregg's sister, Aunt Gen and Uncle Charlie. But as I got older, gifts from parents seemed less fun, often just clothes to wear. My parents couldn't afford the neat things that my peers got under their tree. At times, I felt jealous and often deprived.

Cliff Recalls Childhood Christmases with Relatives

Every few years my grandparents came to visit, and I remember at least once that my mother's sister, Aunt Alice Hinkle came with her husband Uncle John with their two boys. Uncle John was a farmer and also drove big rig trucks. Father and sons were usually about twice their suitable sizes and wore bib overalls. Maybe one of Dad's sister, Aunt Lois came, but I'm not even sure of that. So, we were sort of out in a far country when it came to socializing with family.

Going to Grandma's filled us with glee. On Christmas Eve before we left for Camas, my dad packed the backseat of our tan Dodge with layers of clothing until they came up to the level of the rear passenger seats. As young kids, the beefed-up back seat became a little play area all our own. It was there that my siblings and I would play games, rest or sleep on top of blankets and pillows as my dad drove west across the state.

Christmas morning began about 3:30 a.m. We would all get dressed and share presents around the Christmas tree. There was usually teasing and some goofy present for my dad for example, an old smelly shoe all wrapped up with a beautiful bow). At 4:00 we headed for Grandma's, my dad's mother on Southwest Park Street, along the Columbia River. There were no interstate roads in those days, so the trip took several hours. About midway, we usually stopped for a short break at Ginkgo Petrified Forest to stretch our legs. We munched on fruit, snacks and sandwiches in the back seat of the car, sometimes playing the game of how many out of state licenses we could find as the cars passed us. Washington State law during those years required displaying a license tag on both the front and rear of the vehicle.

My Dad's goal was to arrive in Camas around lunch time to have a great big meal and reunite with my Grandmother Alice Gregg and our step-Grandfather, Grampa Gregg, all the cousins, aunts and uncles, a joy-filled experience.

After the meal we cousins would disappear in our age groups and explore the orchard or woods. We took turns swinging on a tire from a long rope attached to a neighbor's huge fir tree. Often, I'd climb up to a rock formation I named The King's Seat, to get a glimpse of the Columbia River. Later the gang reappeared for dessert and gift exchange. How did the relatives exchange gifts? Well, during the previous Christmas individual names in appropriate age groups were written on a small piece of paper and put inside Grampa Gregg's hat. We would each pick out a secret name and think about next year's Christmas present for that person. After Christmas time with the large family gathering, we would drive back the long road to Spokane, isolated from relatives once again.

My Checkered Life: A Marriage Memoir

Part 2

Marital Happiness and Hassles

"A miraculous event unfolds when
we throw the lead of our personal story into
the transformative flames of creativity.
Our hardship is transmuted into something golden."

– Richard Rohr, *Fallow Time*

My Checkered Life: A Marriage Memoir

Chapter 11

Our Wedding: The Mothers Meet

A cloche of white netting flocked with tiny appliqué blossoms covered Viola Beaman's honey-blonde curls on our wedding day. Standing tall, and no doubt at the photographer's instruction, she held the ribbony end of my bridal bouquet, and my prayer-veiled mother held the trail of flowers on the other end, a cascade of white carnations and roses bridging the gap between the mothers of bride and groom. Mother Ruth, age fifty, wore a long-sleeved, blue-caped crepe dress and Mother Viola, three years younger, a blue and pink floral, sleeveless. I remember ordering a pink carnation corsage for Mother which would match the pink pastel of the bridesmaids' dresses. She'd look less plain too.

My parents liked Cliff. Although my husband-to-be was not Mennonite, they approved of him. They enjoyed his sense of humor and the fact he was already launched in a career. After all, their daughter was now twenty-six years old, and they sensed she knew her own mind. My mother told me while we were dating, "I'd rather have you be a happy Christian than a sad Mennonite." When Cliff asked for my hand in marriage, my dad queried, "Can you support her?" Cliff answered "Yes," but we both knew it would take both incomes to launch us successfully into married life and save to buy our first house.

Bridal shower thank you note

11 – Our Wedding: The Mothers Meet

Mother Longenecker and Vi Beaman Wedding portrait

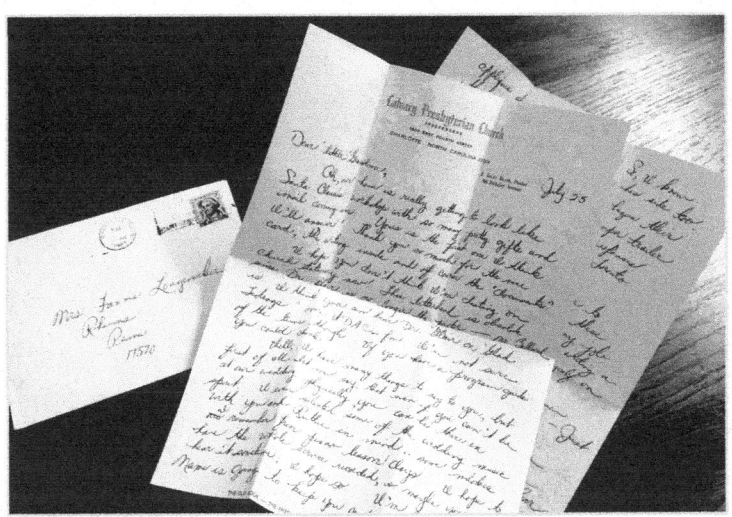

My Letter to Grandma, dated July 27, 1967, refreshed my memory about some events I had forgotten

My Checkered Life: A Marriage Memoir

Chapter 12

Marriage Ceremony

Just over a year and half after we met in December 18, 1965, Cliff and I stood before the pastor of Calvary Presbyterian Church in Charlotte, North Carolina, and pledged our troth with words adapted from the Book of Common Prayer. It was August 5, 1967.

As we stood, we promised before God to love and cherish . . . to honor . . . to sustain in sickness *as* in health, in poverty *as* in wealth, in the bad that may darken [our] days, in the good that may lighten [our] way, *and* to be true. I did not promise to obey my husband. Why would I need to do that if I loved, honored, and remained true to him?

The pastor, Dr. Dean B. Ballard intoned, "Then you are devoted to each other until death parts you." He was insistent that we use the phrases "in sickness *as* in health, in poverty *as* in wealth."

I have a sharp recollection of his saying to me, as his secretary that summer typing the words of our vows, "It's easy to stay together when you are both healthy and financially stable, but watch out when sickness visits your home, or lack of money lurks at your door." I am reminded of Wendell Berry, in his essay *On Poetry and Marriage* who affirms that "The meaning of marriage begins in the giving of words. We cannot join ourselves to one another without giving our word."

Kneeling at the altar before the wedding prayer, noted in Chapter 38, Compensation: A Wedding Anniversary Meditation

12 – Marriage Ceremony

A joyous ressional

The wedding service itself was a blur. I remember thinking as the rear doors opened and I paused on my father's arm facing the altar, "My life is never going to be the same after this." I reminded myself to cherish every moment of our ceremony, which I recall now as feeling surreal, an out-of-body experience. At one point, I thought I might faint though I was leaning on a strong arm.

After the recessional, Cliff and I had a few moments to ourselves in the vestibule before we lined up with parents and bridal party in the reception line. He jumped up from the carpet, bouncing on his rented black patent leather shoes, "It's legal now. It's LEGAL!" What he meant was that now we could legitimately have sex. I wanted to correct him and say, "You mean, 'It's moral (or ethical),'" but it felt so wrong to squelch his exhilaration by inserting sensible words.

12 – Marriage Ceremony

My Checkered Life: A Marriage Memoir

We were married on August 5, 1967, not on August 6 as penned on the page

12 – Marriage Ceremony

My Checkered Life: A Marriage Memoir

Chapter 13

The Engagement: A Flashback

We had gotten engaged the Christmas before, December, 1966. At the time, I was teaching senior English in North Carolina at Charlotte Christian School. Cliff was teaching sixth grade at Norwood School in Jacksonville, Florida, and serving as youth pastor at Fellowship Bible Church. He proposed as we parted just before New Year's, "I'm going to write a letter to you every day, and I'd like you to do the same." He wanted to have something to cheer him up after a grueling day teaching, a job he was not prepared for and disliked, and I liked the idea of writing to stay in touch. After all, we were saving to get married, and long-distance phone calls cost money. My room-mate, Anne, was not as enthusiastic about our extreme letter-writing. Anne, who retrieved the mail from the metal box attached to the wall on the front porch every day, told me a few times, "I wish John would write oftener." With those pouty words I imagined her placing Cliff's letter grudgingly on the coffee table when the mail came. My other room-mate Sally had a beau who lived in town, up close and personal. Once, Sally and I went to hear Dr. Martin Luther King speak, an event I labeled "Exciting!" in my journal of September 23, 1966, not imagining then the impact of his untimely death in May 1968. Both women helped me navigate the tricky transition from my provincial Mennonite culture in Pennsylvania to a wider world, showing me the how-to of hair rollers for a flip hair-do, applying hair spray and touches of rouge and cherry-red lipstick.

Maybe because of the mystique of our differences or because we had similar interests, ours was a whirlwind romance sustained by letters for months after Cliff returned to post-graduate work and me to teaching. Then his letters dwindled, probably because of his hesitation about dating a girl like me from such a strange background. *Would she take off her prayer cap?* And, *Would she wear a diamond ring?* he wondered.

In March 1966 he confessed he wasn't sure he loved me. He wanted to revert back to his old habit of cherry-picking girls for dates in college.

Then he slapped me with s rejection, "I guess I need to play the field again." During college days he had a little black book in which he entered names of girls that interested him. After they passed the sensational-physical-attributes test, their names were entered into this book. He told me some girls' names were crossed off the list because they were too giggly, walked like a duck, or were unable to sing on key.

13 – The Engagement: A Flashback

Cliff-hanger Moments

My boyfriend went into comparison shopping mode again as he began his first-year teaching, dating a nurse from a fine family. I was devastated, knowing he was The One. In May of the same year I wrote in my journal: "Sometimes the night rain does a better job of crying than I do. Its Kleenexes are so absorbent. Even the stars can disappear without exposing puffy eyes the next morning." In the next sentence I wrote, censuring myself, "This is the most morbidly pathetic thing I ever wrote." Months later, he said after he had come to his senses, "I couldn't get you out of my mind. I thought I would miss something if I said goodbye to you forever."

According to Cliff, two things I did sealed the deal for him. I made him a monogrammed bath robe for Valentine's which kept him from freezing on off-campus housing his last few months in college. Also, I called various hospitals to try to figure out in which hospital he was a patient when he had pneumonia and was too sick, or too uninterested, to contact me.

Fortunately, our friendship was rekindled when we both attended the August 1966 wedding of the couple who introduced us, Paul and Betty Mumma. Soon Christmas rolled around again, and Cliff drove from Jacksonville, Florida, to pick me up in Charlotte, where I was teaching. From there we headed to my hometown, in Pennsylvania in his white Plymouth Savoy.

There one snowy evening before Christmas, Cliff suggested "Let's take a drive." So, we bundled up and headed out, crunching footprints in the new fallen snow. Fat flakes were falling from the sky even thicker as we slid into the car, the plastic seats crackling from the cold. Memories of the evening have become a movie in my mind.

"Where are we going?" I quizzed.

"Oh, I don't know. We'll just take a drive in this beautiful snow," Cliff replied rather nonchalantly.

As he tried hard to urge the heater to warm us up, we reminisced about our first dates the Christmas before. "Do you remember how deep the snow was when we went to see The Sound of Music?"

Of course, I do!" The car's windshield wipers were swishing away mini-cotton balls of snow now.

In the back of his mind, Cliff wondered, "What will she say if I ask her to marry me?"

As we approached the archway between Rheems and Mount Joy, I exclaimed, "The road hasn't been plowed any farther. We're at a standstill!" We had come to a crossroads.

Then he said, "If you thought it was God's will, would you marry me?"

13 – The Engagement: A Flashback

Quickly I responded, "Of course I would." But instantly I recognized this as a marriage proposal encased in a tricky question, a snowy fleece.

"Well, then, will you marry me?"

I don't know why he thought he needed a safety-net question as a prelude. I had given every indication of willingness to accept when the question came.

With a "Yes," the camera in my mind dissolved into hugs and kissing, definitely more intense than a Hallmark movie ending.

And yes, his little black book has been destroyed long ago.

Cliff's Story: Rabbits and Rings

I proposed to Marian my Mennonite girlfriend one snowy evening in 1966, my car stuck in a snow-bank. When she accepted my proposal, I also asked her, "Would you be willing to wear a ring?" This is the plain girl I have fallen in love with: no make-up, no jewelry, especially no ring on her finger, ever.

Now it was close to Easter and Marian flew from Charlotte to spend the weekend with me in Jacksonville. Technically, she would be with me most of the time though she will spend the night at Mom and Pop Rea's house, members of the church where I served as youth pastor. No sleeping together before marriage. While their son was away, serving in the Viet Nam war, the Rea's become my surrogate parents. Petite and handy in the kitchen and at the sewing machine, Mom Rea could make the best carrot cake ever and upholster large pieces of furniture like nobody's business. Pop Rea, large and gangly, wore bib-overalls and compensated for hearing loss, cupping his hand over his ear. "How's that?" he'd ask. A carpenter by trade, he lost his middle finger in an accident, an appendage he referred to as a "thin-ger." Though his hair was sparse, he appreciated the occasional haircut I gave him.

I'd been wracking my brain to find a way to make the ring presentation unforgettable—and a surprise too. "So, this is what I'll do. I'll make a ham dinner for her, finishing it off with dessert, a cake with her engagement ring baked inside. No, wait! A cake is too big; the ring may get lost in it. I'd better make cupcakes or muffins."

Her Story:

Charlotte had been my home in the 1966-67 this school year, but with every stitch of my wedding gown. I dreamed of my life with soon-to-be-husband Cliff in Florida. During Easter weekend in March 1967, I took an Eastern Airlines flight to Jacksonville. The carefree, goofy guy I had fallen in love with had hit real life, teaching sixth-graders, some unruly, in an inner-city school. He had also exchanged a college dorm for a $ 50.00 per month, second-story garage apartment with a turquoise-teal kitchen, where I will live after our honeymoon.

13 – The Engagement: A Flashback

But his humble abode had not killed romance or his wish to entertain.

We sat down to his home-made ham dinner, which I remember included baked potatoes and lima beans. Cliff, as host, insisted that he clear the table. As he clattered the dishes into the kitchen sink, I looked around from the kitchen/dining area to the very sparse living room space: a reclaimed sofa, which Mom Rea had recently re-upholstered along with a side chair, and something new: a very large Magnavox radio-record player from Penney's with antique grill work on each side. Oh, so I can bring my recordings from my Columbia Record Club membership: "Songs of the West," The Singing Nun, with her "Dominique, Dominique" tune, "Joan Baez in Concert," and Peter, Paul, and Mary vinyl records.

My teeth struck something hard and metallic. Uh-oh. I didn't want to embarrass Cliff by exposing his lack of baking expertise, so I tried to hide the wad of foil under my plate. Eying what I thought was a *faux pas,* he urged, "Why don't you see what's inside?" Cautious but obliging, I unwrapped the layers and layers of foil. As I peeled back the last piece of blackened foil, something gleamed back at me. My eyes popped with pleasure–a glittering diamond solitaire, my first ring ever. My dear betrothed had gone to the trouble of making some rabbit cutouts with toothpicks, blue for him and red for me, so he'd know which muffin the ring had been baked in. I was dazzled—by the diamond ring *and* by the unique presentation.

Postscript

About five years later after I became a young mother, I removed the ring to apply lotion to my hands, placing it on a top of the bedroom dresser. What happened later occurred out of sight and only in my reconstructed memory: Three-year-old daughter Crista must have found the ring and put it on a chubby little finger. Wearing it to go potty, she flushed my sparkly diamond down the drain. Screams ensued. Cliff digs frantically into lawn soil hoping the ring has gotten lodged somehow in the trap of the drain pipe before flowing into the Neverland of the city sewer . . . to no avail.

13 – The Engagement: A Flashback

My Checkered Life: A Marriage Memoir

Chapter 14

Wedding Guests and the Reception

I was surprised how many friends and relatives from my hometown attended our wedding. These hardy souls from Lancaster County drove the long distance that hot August weekend from southeastern Pennsylvania to Charlotte, North Carolina. We were touched by their presence.

Just now I'm looking at a photo of my Aunt Ruthie, Grandma Longenecker, and her sister Sue Martin, along with Grandma's neighbor Anna Groff who all came for the wedding, standing in front of the gray bungalow I shared with roommates the previous year. Three plain ladies and one fancy one, Sue, look eager to take the short drive to the church where Billy Graham's mother "Morrow" was a member. My dad who was enamored with Billy Graham and his ministry at the time, and may have hyped up the fact that his daughter was getting married in the "Graham" church as a lure to get hometown folks to attend. As a matter of fact, my Aunt Ruthie and Grandma Longenecker were thrilled and honored to stay as guests in the home of Mrs. Morrow Graham while they were in Charlotte, a kind gesture. Her sturdy, brick dairy farmhouse was also the site of a bridal

Aunt Ruthie, Grandma Fannie, Anna Groff and Sue Martin leaving Middleton Drive house

shower my roommate Anne had thoughtfully planned for me a month earlier, the guests all new women friends I met as I transitioned from my plain to a "fancier" life.

Other attendees from Pennsylvania represented three segments of my life then: Miriam Hess from Bossler Mennonite Church, John Herr and wife Joann, who accompanied me earlier on a trip west, colleague Verna Mohler [Colliver] and then Dean of Girls Alta Hoover [Ranck], and friends from

14 – Wedding Guests and the Reception

10A—THE CHARLO

MRS. BEAMAN

Longenecker-Beaman

Miss Marian M. Longenecker of 121 Middleton Dr. and Clifford D. Beaman of Jacksonville, Fla., were married Saturday in Calvary Presbyterian Church. The Rev. Deane B. Ballard officiated at the 2 p.m. ceremony.

The bride is the daughter of Mr. and Mrs. Ray M. Longenecker of Elizabethtown, Pa. She is a graduate of Eastern Mennonite College and taught last year at Christian High School. She is secretary to the pastor at Calvary Presbyterian Church.

Mr. Beaman, the son of Mr. and Mrs. Lee A. Beaman of Vancouver, Wash., is a graduate of Bob Jones University where he joined Phi Kappa Pi Society. He is associate pastor of Fellowship Bible Church, Jacksonville, and teaches in the Jacksonville public schools.

The couple will live in Jacksonville after a trip to Asheville.

Lancaster Mennonite School, where I had previously taught English.

Cliff's parents and sisters Joyce and Kathy took a northern route in a red and white Ford camper, driving all the way from Washington state. They passed through Detroit, Michigan, during the race riots that year. They had not been keeping up with the news, and had no idea Detroit was a hotbed of racial discontent in 1967. In fact, when they took a short lunch break and pumped gas, Joyce apparently hadn't gotten back into either the cab or the camper area of the pickup, and somehow got left behind. Someone must have said, "Where's Joyce?" and discovering her missing, had to retrace the miles, and drive right back into streets with flaming businesses and gunfire to retrieve their missing daughter.

My Checkered Life: A Marriage Memoir

Then came the reception. It was a modest affair with mints, peanuts, cake and punch. In fact, the whole wedding was on the cheap. My teaching salary of about $ 3500.00 was stretched to pay for most of the expenses. I was on a pay-as-you-go, no-credit-card system. Today's Bridezillas would freak out at my teeny tiny budget for a church wedding. Ever the list-maker (call me OCD), I began my planning with a double-columned list: item + amount spent. My gown made from a Simplicity pattern cost

$83.05, the invitations, $95.70. The cake, flowers, napkins, and photographer were also part of the budget. I was not very good, however, at justifying my bank balance. I remember standing in front of a teller at Wachovia Bank unable to choke back tears at my overdrawn account just weeks before the wedding.

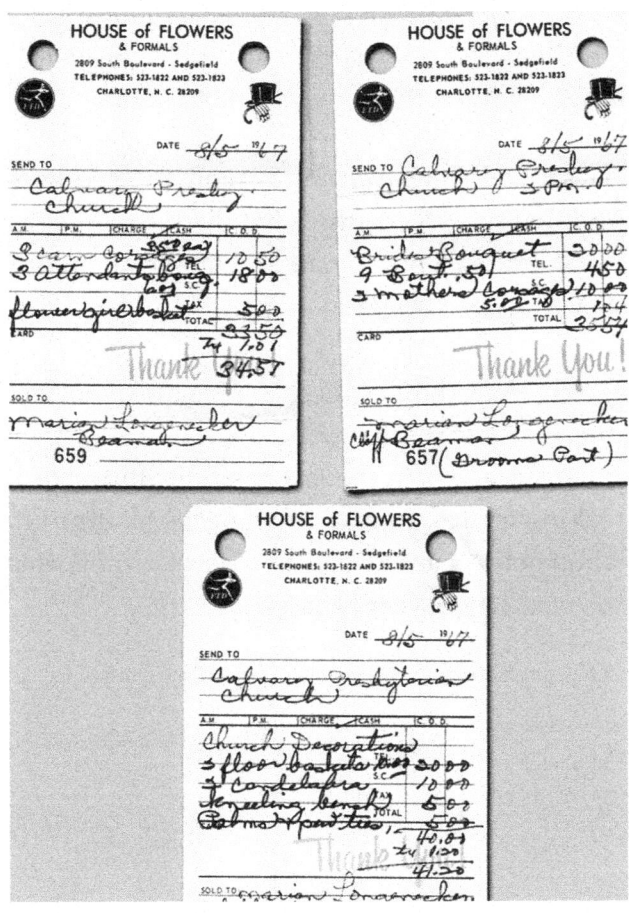

Another time I wanted to choke back tears happened when I approached the custodian with my paltry tip for his arranging tables and chairs for the reception in fellowship hall. Still in my bridal finery, I handed him a check for his services. He extended his arm hopefully, then looked at the amount and blurted out, "But I spent a lot of time setting up and making sure everything was up to par." I don't remember the exact amount of the check I gave him, but it was probably only a fraction of what he was used to getting.

"I'm sorry, sir. I don't have any more money to give you. I wish I did." And that was the truth. What distressed me most was the fact that he was a black man and maybe thought I didn't believe he deserved a proper payment.

You may ask, "Why didn't Cliff help ease the financial burden of wedding expense?" My groom labored like a stevedore all summer long, a rigger in the Jacksonville Shipyards hauling back-breaking chains up and down decks to afford the honeymoon and get us launched as newlyweds in his apartment before the next school year began.

14 – Wedding Guests and the Reception

My Checkered Life: A Marriage Memoir

Chapter 15

Our Honeymoon and Camping in the Smokies

Asia Wong, author Ada Calhoun's therapist, offers sage advice to newlyweds—to old marrieds as well: " ... you need to figure out how to build sway into a marriage, the way you do into the foundation of a building. She [Asia] says that just as a tall building or bridge without room to expand or contract, to move in stiff winds, falls down, so a marriage that's too rigid crumbles at the first tremor." (from *Wedding Toasts I'll Never Give*).

Yes, we had tolerated tiffs during our courtship, even survived a break-up, but now we were *married*. We held a marriage certificate signed by the church officiant and our attendants, sealed by Mecklenburg County in Charlotte, North Carolina. A contract. A commitment for life.

I tossed my beribboned bouquet to a hopeful bridesmaid, and Cliff and I dodged a rain of rice as we descended the church steps. We hopped into the groom's white Plymouth sedan, adorned with a white banner covering the entire trunk, announcing in big, white-on-black letters JUST MARRIED and headed to Middleton Drive. We drove to the gray house with a bay window and two-dormers that I would leave for the very last time. If pranking groomsmen had tied tin cans to the back bumper, we were unaware. We were hearing wedding bells. I entered the door with my Jackie Kennedy-inspired bridal gown and left with a cool, summery yellow "going away" suit made of soft challis, another hand-made outfit I loved wearing, a sheath dress with a fitted jacket. The "exit dress" or special going-away outfit is obsolete now, but in the 1960s it was *de rigeur* for brides traveling with their new husbands to a hotel for the wedding night.

Facing the warm afternoon glow, we headed the 130 miles toward Asheville, North Carolina, in Cliff's dad's "limousine." The elder Beamans' wedding gift to us was a gas credit card and the use of their red Ford pickup truck with a white topper. The topper, a fiberglass canopy covering the pickup's rear bed, supplied a raised mattress for sleeping and storing suitcases and camping gear, a Coleman lantern, ice chest and stove. The outfitted truck was their lodging on the long journey from Washington state to Florida. Now it would be our traveling "nest," an economical way to honeymoon in the Smokies, two newlyweds on a shoe-string budget.

"Here we are!" Cliff exclaimed, after parking in front of the Holiday Inn for a one-night stay. He brought in two suitcases, his big and clunky, and mine a small, ancient plaid cardboard

15 – Our Honeymoon and Camping in the Smokies

suitcase, featherweight in comparison. He came back to the passenger side of the camper and nestled me into his arms and headed toward the entrance. "I want to do this right," lifting me over the door's threshold. Grinning with delight, he announced, "We're legally married now!"

He sniffed, opening the door of the motel gingerly, "It smells decent," relieved he wouldn't have to put up with a foul odor from a previous smoker that might trigger an asthma attack. He brought in two suitcases, his and hers, hefting them over the threshold, no wheels or long handles in those days.

Leaving for supper in Asheville

My Checkered Life: A Marriage Memoir

Our supper may or may not have been candle-lit. I don't remember, but I do recall taking a hot bath, spritzing my body with Estée Lauder cologne and then getting all dolled up in a pure white peignoir set. I must have looked like a present ready to be unwrapped in my filmy lace and silk nightie, a satin ribbon tied in a bow around my waist. The look on my new husband's face confirmed that I wouldn't disappoint him.

My hymen was broken, pierced by an ardent but tender mate, consummating our marriage. I noticed a blood stain on the white sheets the next morning. Although I knew the maid service could take care of the red spot after they stripped the bed, I rubbed cold water on it, so it would look less conspicuous.

"Dear, next time leave the bacon in a little longer. I like it done but not crispy." I was standing in front of the camp stove from Sears, which sat on a wooden table at the campsite, the sizzling bacon resting on a rolled-up paper towel.

"Okay," I complied, breaking four eggs into the hot grease for breakfast in the wilds. My previous experience cooking meals was taking turns making supper for roommates in an off-campus trailer at Lancaster Mennonite School, and then in the little house in Charlotte. We sometimes repeated recipes when it was our turn to cook. I remember often making the chicken-rice casserole dish with onion soup mix and a can of mushroom

15 – Our Honeymoon and Camping in the Smokies

soup, Anne and Sally's favorite. Now I had a husband to please, someone who didn't have a ladylike appetite.

I was wearing a plaid, checkered jacket thick with the tang of bacon, the Smoky Mountains cool in the morning. It was the third day into our honeymoon. We had shopped at the Piggly Wiggly in Asheville the morning after our wedding night: bacon, eggs, bread, cold cuts, lettuce, tomatoes, peaches, two rolls of paper towels and plates on the shopping list.

Honeymooning and hiking sucks the energy out of you, especially if you can't get a decent night's sleep. We were, after all, in the mountains, on an incline. It was hard to find a level spot to park the camper. And we moved almost every day. I realized I had married a true pioneer, an explorer. *What's on the other side of this mountain?* he wondered. His ancestors must have ridden across the continent bouncing along in stagecoaches more than a century ago, filled with wanderlust, shouting "Giddyap!" I would have been content to stay two or three days at the same site. But, no, "Let's go to Clingman's Dome tomorrow. It's over 6600 feet high. We'd have our heads in the clouds!"

My head wasn't in the clouds anymore. Being married to a super-energetic guy was going to be *work*. It was hard to keep up. We did scale part of Clingman's Dome, and I have a picture of my husband leaning against a brown forestry sign at the top, the observation deck at the summit. He actually did look tired too. Leaning slack against the sign, it appeared as though one of the wooden posts was holding him up.

But not tired enough to slow the pace. We rode a gondola on a Smoky Mountain ridge and visited the Biltmore House back in Asheville. Then north to Gatlinburg, Tennessee, and down to Little Jerusalem Lake in South Carolina, ending up on Florida's west coast near St. Petersburg.

"The mosquitoes are eating me alive! I have had enough of this. Let's go home. Now!" I was exasperated, hot, and exhausted. The honey that had been slowly draining out of the honeymoon for me was completely gone. Of that, I was sure.

15 – Our Honeymoon and Camping in the Smokies

When we got back to Jacksonville, my new home base, we got quite a greeting. "Where have you been?" his parents exclaimed. "We had no idea when you were coming back. It's steamy hot in your apartment. We want to get back home."

My new in-laws had been cooped up in the apartment with no window air conditioner. It never occurred to Cliff to make a short phone call updating his family on our where-abouts or approximate return date. We found out later that we had been gone so long that Cliff's dad had run out of money and had to get a short-term job as an electrician to fund the return trip. The gas card changed hands in short order, and the older Beaman family reclaimed their camper and headed back west to the comfort of a Washington state summer.

I felt embarrassed about all the miles we had logged. Even though gas was 28-30 cents per gallon in those days, we must have racked up quite a bill. Yet Cliff's dad never complained. Not that we were aware.

The clash of the cultures had begun. A young wife whose only experience of camping was Laurelville Mennonite Camp with cabins and a dining hall serving food cafeteria-style was matched with a man whose family exuberantly camped in the wild. In tents. With a gas stove and a Coleman lantern, roughing it.

My husband already lived in a garage apartment in Jacksonville, Florida's east side, when I joined him near the end of August 1967. The affordable apartment sat on top of a garage behind the house where our landlady, Mrs. Matyka lived. Every weekend, her son raced his car around her circular driveway in a drunken swirl. Twenty outdoor steps with worn treads led up to the door that opened to a turquoise-painted kitchen with a chrome and vinyl dinette set, and then a living room, bedroom and tiny bathroom. Cliff told me that I should expect to put our clothing in cardboard boxes. Earlier I had the crazy notion that living with my lover out of cardboard boxes would be romantic, but I was surprised and relieved when he showed off some sturdy walnut furniture, a dresser and chest of drawers from Haverty's furniture store, a suite we still use to this day.

Cliff and Marian: Teaching Careers

On the first day of school before Labor Day, I watched my husband descend the stairs outside, his tan slacks slapping against his long legs going off to his sixth-grade class at Norwood Elementary School. Even though a few minutes later, I would set off for Robert E. Lee High School, I felt abandoned. Left behind. Oddly, I thought of the verse in Deuteronomy 24:5. Although I couldn't remember the exact reference in that moment, I did recall the essence: "If a man has recently married, he must not be sent to war or have any other duty laid on him. For one year he is to be free to stay at home and bring happiness to the wife he has married." (paraphrase, *The Message*). This was Old Testament wisdom, though, not applicable to young marrieds living paycheck to paycheck.

15 – Our Honeymoon and Camping in the Smokies

After the day-to-day intimacy on our honeymoon, I should have been happy to be alone. To have some breathing space. And yet. Call it ambivalence. I was in a large city of over 250,000, needing to navigate strange streets and avenues by myself. Lee Senior High was located in what was then an affluent part of town. The English teachers looked proper and "old school," especially the department chair, Mrs. Goethe. One of the teachers wore her hair pompadour style with a twist-up roll around her neck, very 1940s looking. Except for the rather pink and round Mrs. Gaffney, cheery with a halo of fluffy white hair and joyous smile, the department looked quite staid.

"I'm going to visit your class today, Mrs. Beaman, so you won't be shocked when I open the door. I'll sit in the back for a short while." I suspected Mrs. Goethe thought I couldn't keep order. After all, I was new to the department, and to her must have looked young and perhaps inexperienced. After only one visit, I think she realized I had the students' attention and was up to the job. It's strange that looking back on more than forty years as a successful educator, moments like these come alive in my memory, and I smile. I thrived teaching Greek myths and Mark Twain in ninth-grade English, putt-putting back and forth from our apartment on Thirtieth Street to the campus on McDuff Avenue in my old gray Valiant, its exhaust pipe puffing-out purple smoke.

Snakes! I do hate snakes. As a child, I couldn't even look at pictures of them in Aunt Ruthie's *Geographic* magazines. I was familiar with silver fish too, little hairy slivers, scurrying around in a drawer where household bills were stored in my childhood home. Ants were common too as were flies swarming around fresh corn and peaches during canning season. A sticky honey-colored ribbon suspended from the ceiling usually took care of those pesky plagues.

But the cockroaches of the South—oh, my word—how wretched! With six long spiny legs, and a flat, oval-shaped brown body with wings, they scuttled along our floors and around plumbing. Even keeping dirty dishes out of the sink and crumbs off the floor didn't deter them. We shot them with *RAID,* but they scampered away only to re-appear.

Our first semester together was trying in other ways too. Tired from a week of teaching, Cliff spent Friday nights with kids. As youth pastor of a small church in Jacksonville's Northside, he was used to organizing young people for costumed skits illustrating Bible stories, a Halloween event staged near a cemetery, and trips to the zoo. At first, I was a good sport, joining in wholeheartedly. But after a few months, I was worn out. Exhausted. To tell the truth, beyond exhausted. My stomach started doing flips. I lost weight. By Thanksgiving, I was done. I wasn't up to festive preparations of any kind. Cliff bought a twenty-pound turkey that he filled with herbed stuffing. "I bought a big turkey. Think of all the nice leftovers we can have. We'll have enough to freeze!" I was thankful he was game to play chef as I was scheduled to have two of my wisdom teeth pulled during the short holiday.

He had wonderful intentions to use the meat for sandwiches and soup, but a week later, we smelled a foul odor. "I wonder what's dead around here," we mused. "A rat? I haven't seen any rats or mice scurrying around." Eventually one of us opened the oven

15 – Our Honeymoon and Camping in the Smokies

door. A horrible stench emanated from the square cavity as we beheld a decaying turkey. Neither of us remembered to refrigerate the bird after our Thanksgiving feast, just for the two of us.

Our first year held other surprises, one of them a miscarriage. Although I was taking birth control pills, I became pregnant and lost the unplanned baby before the third month. The doctor explained my hemorrhage: "The fetus will pass through your body naturally, but you should take it easy for a while. Probably there was something genetically wrong, and it's a good thing it happened before you got more advanced." I wasn't so sure. I felt empty and sad for a while, but then secretly relieved because we were saving to buy our first house.

We secured our first house on the Southside of the city for $14,500, with a $2500.00 loan from my generous mother and father-in-law Beaman, a sum which we paid back regularly with interest. It was a cute three-bedroom, two-bath concrete-block rancher with gray stone insets and white shutters. Our daughter, Crista Joy, was born at Christmas time, two and a half years after our marriage. It was a joyous Christmas. A year later in the same house with a fragrant Frasier fir Christmas tree, our little girl uttered one of her first words, "Pret-ty!" her fat fingers trying to touch one of the shiny globes on the decorated tree.

When Crista was three months old, my Longenecker family visited our home to have a peek at our baby daughter. My seventy-nine-year-old Grandma and my dad and mother flew down from Harrisburg, Pennsylvania, to Jacksonville. A color photo captured four generations beaming proudly at the camera.

*1970, Dad, Grandma, Marian and Crista
in the back yard of Sam Road house*

Chapter 16

Change and Challenge

For five years I noticed Cliff had become increasingly discontent within the four walls of a traditional classroom, first teaching sixth grade in a public school, and then teaching the middle grades in a private school. He invariably turned geography lessons into colorful murals. His English classes featured students' writing and performing plays, not necessarily complying with the standard lesson plan.

During the fall semester one year, ninth grade students were studying motors and engines in their physical science class. One school day Cliff got the bright idea to take his students outside to teach them some basic motor parts. The plan included some practical training in tire changing. He justified his idea with the reasoning, *Every kid, boy or girl, should know how to change a tire, shouldn't they?*

The administration was not so sure. "We think you should stay closer to the curriculum," the principal admonished. "Besides, there could be liability having students outside like that. And did you know one of your students took the distributor cap off a school bus?" So, of course, that was a big problem too.

The question morphed into a confirmation of his failing to comply with a prescribed protocol. Obviously, my husband was getting antsy within four walls. Like the proverbial square peg in a round hole, he struggled to express himself creatively as a teacher, but missing the mark because of the constrictions of a set curriculum.

True, in the past year, Cliff had supplemented his teacher's salary in creating caricatures and realistic sketches for the AnnieTiques restaurant Sunday afternoons at our local mall. In his graphic arts business, he created a slide program brochure for community school publicity in Florida and designed a brochure for a chiropractor, also using cartoons. But his full-time job was still teaching school.

Then opportunity knocked on our door. Loudly and out of the blue. In early 1971 a guest artist with his family of Swiss bell-ringers visited our church. The silver-tongued musician enticed Cliff with the words, "How would you like to tour public schools in the Southeast with an art assembly program you've created from scratch? You could influence thousands of kids for the good!" My husband soaks up challenge and risk like a dry sponge. I have yet to see him daunted by hairpin curves in Kentucky, washed out bridges, Georgia mud, or Carolina windstorms.

16 – Change and Challenge

Cliff and I both recognized this offer as a ticket to his next step, a way to pursue his dream. I reflected back to being mesmerized by his drawing Santa Claus with colored chalk on a blackboard the week we met in 1965. Of course, school kids would love an artist on stage. I had already tasted life as a professional woman and reveled in it. Now, my dream of becoming content as a wife with a fulfilled husband and also a mother was coming true. Our Crista was a toddler, and I was expecting a second child. *What could be better: a family of four with a happy husband?* I did have some misgivings about how our family would fare when Cliff's itinerary moved out of Florida, and he couldn't come home on weekends. At first, though, I concentrated on the short term and didn't think that far ahead.

Cliff's imagination caught fire with fabulous ideas after we signed the contract with Southeast School Assemblies, the entrepreneurial musician getting a cut of the profits. Excitedly, my husband shared with me a rough outline of his plan for the performance. The "History of Art" program would give students an entertaining overview of art history using his made-up cartoon character named Arthur, "Art" for short. The "A" would stand for "Ancient Art," featuring the cave drawings at Lascaux, France. He made up cartoons to fit the cave motif along with an animated Woolly Mammoth and Saber-Toothed Tiger livening the lecture. Leonardo da Vinci, in another animation, parachuted down from the sky in the "R" for Renaissance period, and finally, modern art slides from "T" for Today included Picasso and Mondrian.

With a September deadline looming, Cliff created a mock-up to advertise the shows to schools, the set designed in a triptych shape. The centerpiece on the platform was an 8-foot square rear-view projection screen using a camera with modified lenses for the art slides. One side panel to the left displayed framed drawings, and the other held newsprint for drawing caricatures live with the audience, which turned out to be a highlight of the show. Pre-recorded Moog-synthesized music provided the audio aspect for all the visuals in the show. The artist's costume functioned as part of the entertainment too. In the fall, Cliff performed on stage in purple slacks, a flashy purple, pink, and white tie with a beige, European-cut jacket. And long side burns.

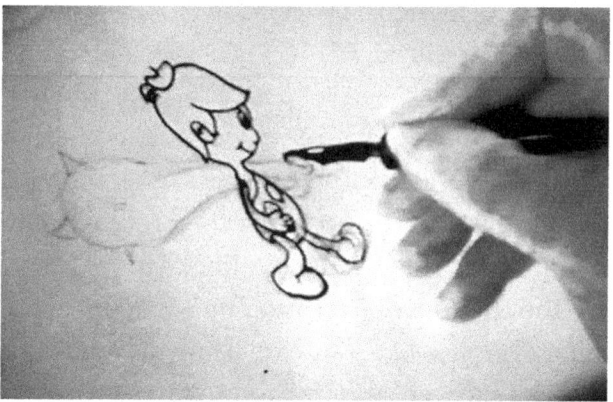

Cliff inking Arthur on acetate over a light box and when flipped over and painted, would become one of many cells to animate with 16mm film

That summer our dining room became a film studio where Cliff selected slides for the show and created animated film. Cluttering the table, crazy equipment like an apparatus from an obsolete X-Ray machine was adapted to become a clunky camera stand to zoom in on each hand-painted cell, an acetate

16 – Change and Challenge

sheet to which acrylic paint was applied. For instance, to depict Arthur as a cave-man walking, nearly twelve individual drawings were required to produce just one second of animation.

Now eight months pregnant, I gambled on whether my husband would have the time to transport me to the hospital. Yes, indeed, in the midst of the scramble to get the "show on the road," our son Joel was born. A few days later in late July, my mother flew down from Pennsylvania to help out with little girl Crista and a newborn.

"Arthur" dressed up as a caveman. Later Arthur was dressed as Leonardo Da Vinci

Somehow, even amidst all of this chaos our precious son was born, Clifford Joel on July 26, 1971. Who knew, maybe this young man would have visual gifts as well. How could he not with a French artist's cap!

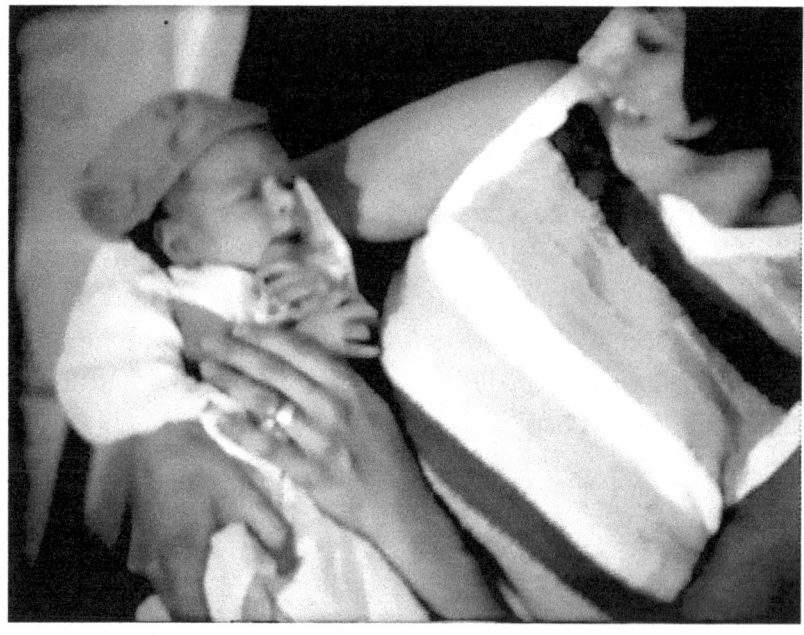

"Oh, my goodness, what in the world is going on here?" Mother exclaimed eying the dining room. Although I had told her about Cliff's new venture, she didn't quite believe her eyes. "Why your house is a 'ferhuddled' mess—and with a new baby, Oh, my heavens!" In addition to the workshop our 1200-square foot house had become, the annoying hammering and sawing in our attached garage to build the "mock-up" was beginning to overshadow the moments of sanity I craved. "Soon the show will be finished, we can clean up, and life will get back to normal after the whole project is done," so I told myself. Was my vision short-sighted? Only time would tell.

The show was totally booked for the full semester before school started. The date for the first show on September 1, 1971, in

16 – Change and Challenge

Sylvania, Georgia, was looming. Now Cliff had to think about actually living on the road. Motels are expensive, so Cliff bought a used 8-foot by 25-foot travel trailer, fortuitously the one our neighbor across the street advertised for sale. In early September, the man, the media, the music, and the mini-home motored down Sam Road into a new adventure. Life settled into a calmer rhythm at home. For a while at least, Cliff came home on weekends, and I, a mother of two, took walks with a toddler and baby carriage, and calmly read bedtime stories in a quiet house.

But the partings on Sunday afternoons were hard for all of us. "Daddy, Daddy, I don't want you to leave," little Crista yelled, flinging herself on the foyer floor, wrapping her arms around her daddy's ankles, and kicking her feet up and down, wailing. Yes, the partings were hard. About a month into the fall season, they became heart-wrenching, especially for our daughter. We had to do *something*.

My Checkered Life: A Marriage Memoir

Cliff introducing his History of Art multimedia performance to one of his K-12 schools thoughout the Southeast United States

16 – Change and Challenge

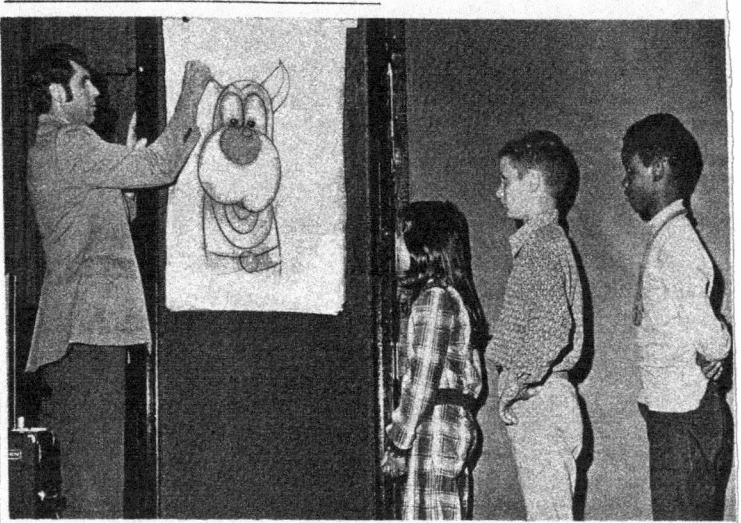

HISTORY OF ART—The Title III fine arts program presented an assembly, "The History of Art," by Cliff Beaman, for students at Scottsburg, Cluster Springs, Sinai, Wilson Memorial and Volens Elementary School May 21-23. Pictured above are Wilson Memorial students (left to right) Jo Ann McDowell, John Terry and John Edmonds with Mr. Beaman as they participated in the assembly, a study of art through cartoon drawings and animations. (Joe Chandler photo)

My Checkered Life: A Marriage Memoir

Chapter 17

The Nomadic Family

"Hel-lo!" I yelled at the woman I saw standing next to a Winnebago on the far side of the campground in the winter of 1972. Our Ford Econoline van and trailer were stuck. The tires whirred, throwing dirt everywhere, sinking deeper and deeper into Tennessee mud. "Can you please help us?" As Cliff bare-handedly scraped loose gravel to throw under the wheels for traction, I trudged red-eyed about two hundred yards to our only neighbor within thirty miles. "We're stuck!"

My appeal for help was met with this: "No, I'm sorry, my husband is recovering from a heart attack and can't exert himself." Turning, I burst into tears—again, feeling stuck in more ways than one.

I was fully behind my husband's new venture at first. I had agreed to signing the contract. Initially I approved because I knew my husband would be happier even though I knew this lifestyle would be disruptive to our family life. At the time, I had only a vague notion of what this decision would entail and how upsetting it would be to our settled, suburban life. The exhilaration I felt at first was quickly wearing off for me.

When Cliff's performance itinerary would no longer allow him to come home on weekends, the babies and I joined his gypsy entourage. I felt like a plant uprooted as we rattled down the street away from our firmly planted house of concrete and timber.

I hated the trailer from the start. To begin with, it was small and scruffy-looking. All of a sudden, my previously grounded life as a thirty-year-old mother had taken on an unfamiliar rhythm: no phone, no mailbox, no fenced-in yard for the children, no feeling of security and very little money. I, this woman, who initially supported her husband in the exhausting months of preparation for the shows, now became an isolated Mrs. Nobody with a remote day-care center. Besides, where do you keep dirty diapers in a confining space? We couldn't afford Pampers. More than once, the green diaper pail decorated with a kangaroo lid and secured with an elastic belt had broken free as we barreled down the highway, sending baby urine yuck all over the teeny linoleum floor.

Before the tour, curious friends asked: *Whose idea was this? Where will you stay? Don't you worry about finding a good doctor? Aren't campgrounds closed in the wintertime?* And then this: *How wonderful! It will bring your family closer together.*

17 – The Nomadic Family

And indeed, it did–a 3-bedroom/2-bathroom household scrunched into a 8' x 25' space required editing and re-orientation of all sorts. How often I wished I could add a chapter to Peg Bracken's *The I Hate to Housekeep Book*. I'd call it "Complete Homecare from the Bed." Just lean over and open the one and only door, shake out the throw rugs and take the broom that's hooked neatly just 3-feet away and sweep. If you angle far enough, you can even take the baby's bottle out of the fridge and swing it to the stove. Keeping a sense of humor helps too.

Joel, Mommy and Crista stepping out of the Ford Van in Manassas, VA just after rain

Our camper was divided into three compartments: kitchen, bathroom and children's bedroom. "Kitchen" was a rough designation for the refrigerator with a portable TV strapped to the top, miniature double-drain sink, gas stove with pots and pans stored in the oven, hinged table that became an instant kiddie sliding board, and finally, a sofa that theoretically made into a smallish "double" bed when the table was dropped into a niche in the wall at night.

"Kitchen" was also the den, living room, dining room, bedroom and occasional art studio. The bathroom was most intriguing. No one had yet invented a lock for a magna-fold door, so forget about privacy with tiny tots. The toilet itself was one of those marine-trap types—no need to worry about Tid-E-Bol. Compare the trap-action at the bottom of the bowl to the springy lid on the mouth of a teakettle. Just press the pedal and "whoosh." And there is absolutely nothing cute I can say about the commode except that our toddler couldn't ladle cups of water out of it. Washer and dryer? Down the road at the Lucky Laundry Spot. And have your quarters ready.

We were cramped in other ways too. The would-be profits kept streaming into the pocket of Cliff's mentor, who had turned from Mr. Silver-Tongue into a Money Bag, which he personally stuffed with our hard-earned cash. I felt immobilized by hatred toward the conniving man who concocted this plan, and who, in my view, took too large a percentage of our income while I felt stuck in a wilderness, literally.

17 – The Nomadic Family

My Checkered Life: A Marriage Memoir

Chapter 18

Night of Crisis

Sometimes the truth we reveal conceals the darker side of a troubling story, even if that story alone seems fraught with hardship. Such is the case with my experience living in a travel trailer with our two small children as my husband Cliff performed his art and music shows through a booking agency in schools. One fateful week in late winter 1973 we camped near Virginia Beach, Virginia. Our daughter Crista had already turned three; Joel was almost a year and a half. I had been isolated for close to two years now, alone in a small trailer with two young children who needed constant care. True, we did spend the previous summer back home in our Jacksonville, Florida house for a few months, but come September it was back on the road confined in an 8' x 25' space again. The second year, finances were as thin as ever, the isolation returned, and I fell deeper into depression. Blinders prevented even a ray of light from penetrating my soul.

One Friday night, with the children in the care of their dad, I walked from the campground, down to the boardwalk. It was late. Neon lights fronting the convenience store flickered weakly, mimicking my feeling of hopelessness. When I walked down the sandy wooden steps leading to the ocean, I heard smashing surf, saw freezing waves and felt the "melancholy long, withdrawing roar" which Matthew Arnold refers to in his poem, "Dover Beach."

Before me the murky Atlantic loomed. The swelling sea called to me. "Just keep walking" it said, the waves lapping like rhythmic arms beckoning me to end it all. Ending my tortured life would bring relief. I imagined I could cross Jordan alone, sinking into numbing oblivion. I wouldn't have to endure life trapped in a confining cage until my husband's contract with the booking agent expired. In my desperate state, even the images of a pony-tailed little girl and her dirty-cheeked brother with mischievous eyes blinking into my consciousness failed to reach me. I kept walking, measuring my steps, my sneaker soles oozing down into the chilly sand. I shuddered. "Wading farther into the water will feel even colder," I realized. Still, "I can't go on like this. Why don't I just end it all?" Now freezing cold water doused the fabric of my sneakers. The mighty ocean could carry me away, and I could disappear, taking the pain with me.

I felt the pull of twin emotions. "I can't do this!"

"Oh, but you can," Despair whispered in my ear. "It would be so easy."

18 – Night of Crisis

"No, no!" my head started to pound.

"End it all, end it all!" the Voice of Hopelessness screamed.

At that moment, "the eternal note of sadness" overtook me, but like the poet, I felt an impulse toward "summoning faith." I pivoted on one soggy heel, turning away from a watery grave. I couldn't go through with my intention to die by drowning.

"What now?" The image of a pay phone I had passed on my way down to the shoreline shone a faint light into my brain. "I'll call Grandma Longenecker," I thought. And so, I approached the black phone on my right, seeming a sentinel of hope, moonlight glinting off the plexiglass shield.

I inserted four quarters into the coin slots in the phone and dialed the familiar number with the 717-area code. "Hi, Grandma, this is Marian."

"Oh, it's so nice to hear from you. Where are you calling from now?" We chatted for as long as I thought the dollar I paid for would allow. I can't recall the conversation, but I don't think we discussed anything grand. And I don't think Grandma ever detected my anguish. I certainly didn't tell her about my suicidal thoughts. But the sound of her voice steadied me. It assured me I was not alone. And I felt some comfort as I ambled back to the trailer, the propane gas-lit windows up ahead beckoning me to return.

Her last question resonated in my ears and gave me an idea: "When you are coming back to Pennsylvania?"

I told her, "I don't know, but I'd like to come soon with the children." Just then it occurred to me if my parents agreed, I could leave the trailer for the two remaining months and save my sanity.

The next morning, a Saturday, I was resolved to confront Cliff with the idea. After dressing in close quarters, we transformed our mattress bed into a couch again and pulled out the tiny table from its storage hatch in the wall. I sat across from my husband, who sensed I was horribly unhappy, his hands outstretched. His concerned expression told me he was trying to read my emotional state.

"I don't want to get a divorce," I said, "but I can't go on like this. I will go completely crazy." Sadness shadowed his face as he reached to hold my tight-fisted hands, his own outstretched. Bridging the gap between us were his hairy arms. Those sturdy arms usually spelled strength and protection to me, but I was beyond those feelings right now. Even if he said "No," I was determined to go ahead with my plan to leave anyway.

"I'm sorry, I know it's been rough, but I wanted to keep the family together. Remember how Crista flung herself on the floor and grasped her daddy's legs when I had to leave at the end of every weekend to do shows?"

18 – Night of Crisis

"Yes, of course I remember, and I did agree to join you with the kids, but I didn't realize how alone I would feel, and I didn't expect we would be so financially strapped for cash." He reached into his pocket, pulling out his wallet: Just a few dollars and some loose change.

So, from March–May, my parents took care of my little brood and me, Cliff coming to see us on weekends. It must have been a sacrifice for my family, but I don't remember them complaining. Crista and Joel did get to know their Longenecker grandparents better, and I could gradually get back my sense of balance and put some weight on my frame that had diminished to 110 pounds.

Cliff honored his contract and finally completed his two-year tour with Southeast School Assemblies in May 1973. During the summer, we put a "For Sale" sign on the travel trailer and settled into our Jacksonville house on Sam Road in Sans Souci, our cozy rancher on a concrete foundation.

As a reflect on this crisis that happened in our marriage more than fifty years ago, I can tell you that isolation is a mental cancer that can eat one's soul alive. Isolation can also lead to depression. In the challenges that would follow, I learned again and again that there is no shame to admit helplessness and seek a way out. Over and over, I have done that. And I have anchored my soul on the coastline of the "sea of faith."

It was not my time to cross Jordan back then. My time will come, though. But I know now that when it does, I won't have to cross Jordan alone.

My Checkered Life: A Marriage Memoir

Looking Though a Mirror with 20/20 Vision

This journey from decades ago eventually moved my husband into a fulfilling career as a self-employed artist while it showed me that the nomadic life is not for me, a woman originating on stable Anchor Road in the bucolic Pennsylvania countryside. Our little ones, now grown, experienced a fantastic geography lesson, peering through the windshield while seated on my lap or between the driver and passenger seat in the era before car seats. Both kids, big sister Crista , and toddler Joel, could roam free all over campgrounds or fly through the air on a swing-set their dad had attached to the rear end of the trailer, ready for set-up Tinker Toy style if we stayed at a campsite two days or more. We brought along Crista's red tricycle and a stroller, in good weather giving us the run of the campground.

What have I learned? While I wouldn't sign a contract for such an assignment again, I don't regret having weathered the storm of this journey. Then too, the Arctic ice of my unforgiving heart has long since thawed. I understand that bitterness is a steep price to pay for perceived offenses, back then at the hands of Mr. Money-minded Musician. Just as importantly, I can empathize with those whose life is in transition, perhaps feeling uprooted as a result of failing finances or the mortifying loss of a life partner.

I did return to teaching in the 1980s after earning a master's degree, stabilizing our income and helping me forge a professional identity again. A man of his word, Cliff completed his contract with Southeast School Assemblies, after having presented 470 shows. Also, in the mid-1980s, my husband created his own art assembly programs for schools and churches. Under the corporate name, American Art Assemblies, he built the set himself and recorded music which accompanied the evolving images he drew on a 4 x 7-foot easel. He scheduled his own shows all over the United States, from New Hampshire to Florida, California to the Carolinas, performing nearly five-thousand shows in total, tapering off just before the pandemic of 2020.

My journey traversing the southeastern United States for eighteen months had also prepared me for other unexpected adventures that have become springboards to my next steps, among them a contentious host in eastern Europe, the story of whom caught the eye of an editor and happily propelled me into my writing career, blogging weekly and publishing two memoirs.

I do believe that everything in our lives, the good or the bad, can be a bridge to a more meaningful view of life. As poet Mary Oliver mentions in "The Journey," though I have traveled a road full of "fallen/branches and stones," along the way I have found my own voice and the courage to move forward.

To Reflect

A trouble-fraught journey you can recall?

A time you felt cramped, or stuck with a decision that caused hardship?

Story of Jonah

I'd like to tell you another story of crisis, actually two incidents that intertwine, one from the book of Jonah in the Old Testament and another from the poet Carl Sandburg. Traditionally, the story of Jonah begins with the prophet trying to escape his divine mission to warn the people of Nineveh of impending destruction. Perversely, Jonah boards a ship going in the opposite direction. Sailors on board try to avert the disaster which Jonah's disobedience has apparently brought on. They toss him into the sea.

18 – Night of Crisis

Miraculously, God saves Jonah by having him swallowed by a large fish, in whose belly he spends three days and three nights, which some say is a metaphor for Christ's death, burial, and resurrection.

Even though a merciful God spared Nineveh from catastrophe, Jonah became angry because the Ninevites did not receive the judgment he thought they deserved.

Then, "The LORD God prepared a gourd, and made it to come up over Jonah, that it might be a shadow over his head, to deliver him from his grief. So Jonah was exceeding glad of the gourd." Jonah 4:6

When the gourd died, Jonah became depressed, noted in the Old Testament Book of Jonah.

To Reflect

Have you been diagnosed with a serious illness? Are you worried about a wayward child? Has an unexpected bill wrecked your finances?

"Man is born to trouble as the sparks fly upward," the Good Book says. All of us experience setbacks and find it hard to stay in balance.

If you are a writer, maybe the book you painstakingly wrote didn't fly. Maybe you're tired of the endless promotion required.

Perhaps you are physically ill or emotionally challenged.

Sandburg Speaks of Hope

American poet Carl Sandburg may be alluding to the feeling of depression in this excerpt:

Carl Sandburg's *"Smoke and Steel,"* 1922.
From IV Playthings of the Wind 8.

> *If I should pass the tomb of Jonah*
>
> *I would stop there and sit for a while;*
>
> *Because I was swallowed one time deep in the dark*
>
> *And came out alive after all.*

My Story

I often felt blue when my children were younger and my husband and I were beginning our careers. Hormones could have also played a role in my emotional roller-coaster rides. I thought then that a kick to our household finances and help from a maid service would fix my mood.

Fortunately, I have never had to be hospitalized for the "down" feeling, but I sympathize with those who have. There is no shame in admitting the problem or seeking help. Nowadays when I fall into a negative mood, I galvanize myself into action and go into

18 – Night of Crisis

a housecleaning or cooking spree. Sometimes I take a long walk or catch lunch with friends.

Doing for others is also a good tonic. Sending a greeting card or chatting with a friend takes the focus off myself. However, sometimes it is healthy to "ride" the mood and let myself feel sad for a while and not anesthetize myself with drugs. Some researchers have speculated that one reason for the current opioid epidemic is that those addicted do not wish to feel pain of any kind, either physical or psychic.

Feelings of depression, for me, often rise like a wave. I think of it as an emotion to get through, not to deny or dismiss. One way to cope: Breathe deeply as you watch for the wave to peak, notice the wave subsiding gradually and eventually come to an end. Allow, perhaps, for a neutral feeling, which may evolve over time into a small spark of positivity.

Except for clinical depression, the "down" feeling is usually a temporal condition, temporary. For me, belief in the Resurrection, both spiritual and physical, can provide eternal hope.

A Retrospective

We had looked through the marriage mirror together with 20/20 vision after our tour doing programs for Southeast School Assemblies. In the late 1980s, it appeared we both had found our footing: Cliff thriving personally and financially in his own multi-media production, American Art Assemblies, and me happily teaching literature and composition at Florida State College in Jacksonville.

Yes, we understood the Yin-Yang of life: The light with the dark, opportunities often disguised as problems, a couple seeking harmony and balance. As the saying goes, we tried to see a problem as a dragon with a gift in its mouth. According to these lines in Ecclesiastes 3:11, "God had put a sense of divine purpose in our lives, separately and together, sometimes mystified by how our lives were unfolding" (adapted, The Amplified Bible). This checkered life we were living, patches of darks and lights stitched with tight threads, was beginning to reveal patterns, proof we were on a good path together, facing the same direction most of the time. Such commitment, however, does not ensure a trouble-free life as Cliff and I discovered again one Friday in 1994.

18 – Night of Crisis

My Checkered Life: A Marriage Memoir

Chapter 19

Sad Friday: The Story of Daffodils

"I've been robbed!" These are the only words my husband, artist/performer Cliff can utter to himself as he walks toward his Dodge van, noticing that the air-vent window on the driver's side has been pushed in at an odd angle. It's about 4:30 a.m. on Good Friday, April 1, 1994.

Rushing around the vehicle to open the side doors, he begins to take inventory of what's missing: sound equipment including a stereo mixer, a professional-grade tape player, a recorder and at least 150 treasured CDs missing from cases. An envelope with cash–gone. All gone! He walks frantically around the parking lot of the Quality Inn he is about to leave and spotted a black suitcase, which the thieves have thrown into a ravine. Empty!

It was the end of a very productive month presenting 35 multi-media school assembly programs in Florida and

Georgia. Cliff had driven to Nashville, Tennessee, because his next shows were in the Memphis area. He had been looking forward to boarding a 6:00 a.m. Delta flight to come home on Good Friday and spend Easter weekend with his family. This weekend, however, turned out to be a mixed blessing. The splendor of the Resurrection service at church conflicted with the discordant thoughts about his recent loss. Call it a nightmare: Lost equipment, lost musical discs, and lost cash. Just then he remembered malfunctioning hotel parking lights that had probably contributed to thieves finding his van as easy prey. After all, it was Nashville, music city.

After returning to the Nashville airport after Easter to continue his itinerary, he took stock. Though the robbery felt like a violation, a form of rape actually, he could count his blessings: 1. His CD player vital to the music that accompanies his drawing was in a separate case, undisturbed and 2. He had copies of program music at his home base, Jacksonville. He could continue his itinerary.

Yet, the experience, to him, felt traumatic. Still reeling from the impact of the loss of inanimate "friends" that provided the musical score to his chalk drawing on a large easel, he had to soldier on toward St. Louis, Missouri for next week's shows. Behind the wheel again, he popped in a cassette tape, a musical companion on the long hauls between cities: classical music and uplifting hymns, a distraction from the recent robbery. His itinerary took him through Cape Girardeau, Missouri, where Cliff's journal notations begin:

19 – Sad Friday: The Story of Daffodills

The undulating ribbon of asphalt in Interstate 55, the hum of the van engine, rumbling of tires, and rushing air together with the music combined their forces to calm my mind... Now a spot of yellow caught my attention. Was it litter – or something else? The blurry image that I imagine are daffodils soon vanished from my side view mirror.

I keep driving but feel an urgency to turn around. The nest of daffodils keeps calling me. Come back. Don't go another mile. You may miss a special moment in your life, a moment that can put a special gladness in your heart.

Finally, I turn around at the next exit, heading south, as I wonder, How far had I traveled since I saw the flowers? I honestly have no idea, but I retrace my path even farther than I thought necessary to spot those daffodils again.

Cliff gave up and headed north again. Feeling a tug even more insistent, he turned the van around one more time.

Passing over the exit I continue searching, almost holding my breath. My jaw set, my eyes straining for anything yellow.

I nervously look at my watch. I can't believe two hours have passed since sighting those images of hope. Miles and time seem to merge together. My odometer indicates I have traveled 120 miles since first turning back. What was I to do? It was getting late; I had to get to St. Louis soon.

And then I saw it—a flash of golden yellow. My heart leaped with joy—It was there after all, several clumps of daffodils, but I saw two huddled together, spring-like beauties, raising their slender pastel green fingers, lifting golden heads to the heavens!

With that, Cliff's journal entry stops. But it ends on a victorious note. I have saved the dried-up daffodils, one headless, in a blue vase for twenty-one years. And I can't find it in me—at least not yet—to destroy these bedraggled tendrils—evidence of a Bad Friday turned Good!

19 – Sad Friday: The Story of Daffodills

*"And then my heart with pleasure fills.
And dances with the daffodils."*

– William Wadsworth, *I Wander'd Lonely as a Cloud*

To Reflect

Have you ever been robbed?

Or, have you searched and searched for something valuable you thought was lost?

Share your story with someone of another generation.

My Checkered Life: A Marriage Memoir

Chapter 20

It's Not that Easy Being Green

Trouble can erupt on the road, traveling. You can crash, get lost, run out of gas. Get robbed even. But danger can also spring up at home. In your own community.

When our children were in their early teens, our family moved into a neighborhood in Jacksonville, Florida, named Killarney Shores with street names like Emerald Isle Circle, Leprechaun Court, and St. Patrick Lane. The names commemorated the memory of Ireland's famous saint, which I can match with my own story of "keeping it green."

The lurid orange zoning sign meant something, stuck ominously at the edge of the woods where our children used to roam freely, up and down the deep ravines and along a serpentine creek bordering the neighborhood. I have always loved natural beauty, so it is no surprise that one of the items on the wish list for our next address was "a house on a hill with tall trees." A hill with tall trees–a laughable request especially since most of Jacksonville is flat with palm trees bordered by the beach. But our prayer was answered–a huge corner lot with seventeen magnificent laurel oak and live oak trees, some dangling Spanish moss, romantic symbols of the Deep South, nestled in a secret cove just blocks off a busy boulevard.

Yet there was much to fear that November day when I spotted the land use/zoning sign: The memory of the terrorist attack on our nation on September 11, 2001 still overwhelming our minds, our community had to address an encroaching menace much closer to home: Our rural, residential zoning status was being challenged by big box Walmart, who wanted to build a super-center in the forested area 200 feet from our homes. This development would threaten the woods our children had played in, close to the burial site of our family dog, and near a lake by which we moored our canoe, "Killarney Queen."

20 – It's Not That Easy Being Green

First, we had to ask, *"What's really going on here?"* There were trips to the Planning and Development Department downtown with my good buddy Ann. If we were going to fight Goliath, the behemoth of retailers, our tiny neighborhood of sixty-five homes had to be educated. When we weighed in as opposition during the first City Hall hearing, dozens of residents responded to my hastily printed green fliers, which exclaimed, "Attack on our Property Values! Save our neighborhood!" Some neighbors came out of curiosity, a few with animosity, but all with concern for the preservation of the quality of life in our secluded, close-knit neighborhood. I, along with my neighbors, became familiar with a strange new vocabulary: Land Use Amendment Application, Planned Unit Development, Rezoning Ordinance.

Neighbors opened their doors to strategy-planning meetings, furnishing refreshments and dishing up good-will. Residents of all ages, men and women, from up-the-hill met those from around-the-circle . . . as we joined hands in consensus. Even our councilwoman, the gregarious Suzanne Jenkins, joined in, assuring us she would resist a decision to develop the rural residential area into commercial use. By that, we understood she meant she would enable us to stall the change of land use in our favor. At her suggestion, we hired a city planner for big bucks to "give us credibility" she told us.

On April 11, 2002 we had a showdown with the Walmart bigwigs, their cool, professional presentation countered by our-best-we-could-do foam-core display. Residents packed a school auditorium, wearing shamrock buttons that read "Keep it Green." My neighbor Richy recently diagnosed with kidney cancer came to show his support. We all listened to Walmart's company staff show-and-tell session, which extolled the merits of the store to the community, implying the layout would make their 215,000 square-foot presence virtually unobtrusive.

However, when our council-woman, Ms. Jenkins, finally took the stand, we were in for the biggest letdown of all: "Really, you'd be better off if you let Walmart develop the land. The company has deep pockets and can make loads of concessions to you. Why they'll even make a big retaining pond with a lovely fountain to enjoy as you drive by." Then came her threat of bad alternatives. "What if an adult entertainment facility buys the land later? Or a huge liquor store? Then where would you be?" To rub it in, the Walmart people asked for some of our shamrock badges, "to show solidarity in pursuing the green," they said. *Green? Green like money?* we imagined.

In the end, the journey toward a resolution was a zig-zaggy path of uncertainty fraught with the unexpected. It was truly Mr. Toad's Wild Ride, like the Disney attraction, careening through a vibrant countryside and possibly ending in disaster. But we were bound together to face our common foe. The St. Johns River-keeper became a new friend, a neighborhood advocate from a nearby community coached us to anticipate possible next "moves" from City Hall and Walmart. The *Florida Times-Union* ran progress reports, the local TV station featured us on an evening newscast. The process proceeded with fits and starts: rapid action followed by long waits. At the final meeting at City Hall, our small group of about a dozen signed in at 5:30

20 – It's Not That Easy Being Green

p.m. and were heard by the formal City Council at 12:45 a.m., the long wait an obvious attempt to shut us down.

Then neighbor Jim asked, "When will we be heard?" As the minutes ticked by, I hoped nobody in our little group of twelve would give up and walk out. Initially, we were disappointed with the outcome. The decision for land use was ruled in favor of Walmart. Still, our community gained thirteen concessions, including 4.7 acres of conservation easement to compensate partially for the additional impact on traffic and loss of wetlands. And, naturally, the fountain mandated by the retention pond anyway, came with the deal!

In the weeks and months following the showdown at City Hall, our city of over a million gave recognition to our tiny community. Killarney Shores received the Mayor's Award and I, the Outspoken Citizen Award for 2002. Cliff, who was traveling extensively with art shows at the time, submitted photos of more upscale designs for Walmart stores that convinced the powers that be to replace their cheesy-looking layout with a more architecturally pleasing design for our neighborhood.

There is more concrete and asphalt next to our beloved woodlands than we would like, and our community will never be the same. Yet, my neighbors and I learned the importance of teamwork to meet an outside challenge, and throughout the ordeal became true friends.

Yes, Kermit the Frog, is right:

> *"It's not that easy being green;*
> *But green's the color Spring.*
> *And green can be big like an ocean,*
> *or important like a mountain,*
> *Or tall like a tree.*
> *When green is all there is to be*
> *It could make you wonder why, but why wonder why?*
> *Wonder, I am green and it'll do fine, it's beautiful!*
> *And I think it's what I want to be."*

When we moved in years ago, Killarney Shores had a very western European flavor with the origin of many residents reflective of the Irish street names. Now we share care, concern, and meals with Burmese, Bosnian, and Black Americans–folks of all colors, a lovely palette of skin tones: white mingling with tan and mahogany. Symphony member, handyman, business owner, and retirees live side by side. And if an outside threat strikes again, I have no doubt we will present a united front.

As I reflect on this attack on our neighborhood more than twenty years ago, I realize how quickly a community's stability can be upset. My neighbors and I learned how fragile our way of life was when confronted with the Beast of Big Business. But I'm also aware that taking the "United we stand; divided we fall" stance saved us from being swallowed whole by an awesome threat.

20 – It's Not That Easy Being Green

To Reflect

Do you live in a neighborhood where you have noticed changes recently or in the last few years?

How have these changes affected you?

Chapter 21

A Toilet Tissue Tale, Ukraine Style

A challenge my husband and I also faced together and on a broader scope was our trip to Ukraine, a mission of goodwill in April 2011. Toilet paper and lecturer's chalk were two essential items which preceded our arrival in Kiev, Ukraine.

Dozens of toilet paper rolls cushioned the fragile sticks of chalk, needed for the nineteen art and music performances Cliff would present in the public schools of Kiev and surrounding towns. The toilet tissue and chalk were packed in Jacksonville, Florida, to sail on a freighter through the Black Sea and shipped to Kiev several weeks before our arrival.

We traveled to Ukraine at the invitation of Kathy Gould, director of a charity fund, ABC Life, which ministers to children and families. We met Kathy as an 8-year-old girl in a small church in Jacksonville, Florida, where Cliff served as her youth pastor.

Even then, she stood out, memorizing scriptures in a flash and eagerly volunteering to play Mary in one of the Christmas skits, so she could hold Baby Jesus. Blond-haired and bright-eyed, she visited Ukraine on a mission trip in her twenties and immediately fell in love with the culture and the people. She saw need too: Many parents, addicted to drugs or alcohol, often couldn't take care of their children who were sent off to orphanages. Thus, in 1993, she began a ministry to children and families, which included outreach to boys and girls in orphanages.

Arrival in Kiev

21 – A Toilet Tissue Tale, Ukraine Style

Fast forward to 2011: At Kathy's invitation, Cliff volunteered to present nineteen multi-media performances to local schools as a gesture of goodwill using a 4' x 7' easel, with character-building and environmental themes. From the nearly dozen themes available, the school principals in Kiev and Zhitomer and other venues selected these two themes: The Earth, You, and Me (related to respecting our environment) and Choices, discouraging the use of drugs and tobacco. On the easel, artist Cliff drew a mural he created, expanding the theme. Music accompanied the 35-minute shows with lyrics in English. Kathy saw to it that the lyrics were projected on a separate screen in the Russian language above the easel so that the students could simultaneously hear English lyrics, while seeing the Russian translation as the drawing progressed.

This specially built, portable easel was shipped from our city by boat to the Black Sea, where the easel with chalk and toilet tissue was loaded on a barge and transported to Kiev, a three-month voyage which involved transfer from several ports of call. When the equipment arrived, Kathy's crew were a huge help ferrying audio equipment, with the easel and chalks, loading and unloading and driving us from school to school in a black Mitsubishi van.

Cliff with set-up crew after one of 19 performances

And, everywhere we went, the students were smartly dressed: high school girls, aged 14-18 strode confidently in patent leather high heels; the boys wore suits, black and spiffy. They studied English as a second language in the curriculum, and

21 – A Toilet Tissue Tale, Ukraine Style

the principals probably saw Cliff's programs as a boon to their students becoming more fluent.

I knew in advance that Russian was the dominant language in Ukraine, and before we left Florida, I practiced some key phrases, like "Good morning" and "Good afternoon." Students responded to my heavily accented "Dobroye utro" or "Dobreyy den" with knowing smiles, polite, but assuring me that I had missed the mark with the pronunciation. I surely didn't sound like a native speaker.

Though Kathy had forewarned me, I was still surprised at the state of affairs in the bathrooms. In school restrooms, soap was a rarity, and I carried sections of toilet paper in my fanny pack wherever I went and made sure Cliff had a supply in his pocket before the intensive production of set-up and performance began. There was absolutely no toilet paper in any of the school restrooms we visited. Strangely, however, I observed not a whiff of foul odor in the bathrooms or among students in the assembly. We were puzzled. Coming from a country where toilet tissue is considered essential in daily life, I learned that in Ukraine, and probably in many other countries in our world, one can cope without this amenity. What I learned is that students bring their own toilet paper with them, wiping theselves clean as they squat over a hole in the floor, the opening usually surrounded by a ceramic rim.

You may wonder, "What was my role? Was I essential?" I knew I wasn't going to be the star on the platform, nor did I want to be in this case. I saw myself as a messenger of goodwill, greeting students prior to the show—and afterwards, using mostly body language as I directed students to wipe off chalks in preparation for the next performance. Very importantly, I documented the whole experience with photos, capturing the details I might otherwise miss, immersed in a completely different culture for two intense weeks followed by a four-day respite in Crimea by the Black Sea.

American insistence on toilet tissue as essential was highlighted during the COVID pandemic. Early in the pandemic of 2020-2022, when I visited Target in my hometown, shoppers were leaving the store with as many packs of toilet paper as the store would allow. This hoarding didn't surprise me, as I knew early on those rolls of toilet paper were at a premium. "But why was toilet tissue so coveted?" I wondered. "Diarrhea is not a symptom of this particular virus. So why the high demand for toilet paper?"

21 – A Toilet Tissue Tale, Ukraine Style

When I queried a store associate, he remarked, "Yes, everyone is buying toilet paper these days; I'm not sure why. And, can you believe, it's happening globally?"

Perhaps not in Ukraine.

To Reflect

Do you and your mate agree on what kind of toilet tissue you prefer? Whether the toilet paper goes over the top of the roll or underneath?

What hard-to-find item or service did you particularly wish for during the pandemic?

A mural in a village north of Kiev

My Checkered Life: A Marriage Memoir

Part 3

Hilarity and High Emotion

"It's time that we began to laugh and cry and cry and laugh about it all again."

– Leonard Cohen, "So Long, Marianne"

My Checkered Life: A Marriage Memoir

Chapter 22

My Husband's Humor

One of the qualities that attracted me to the young Cliff was his lightheartedness and sense of humor. On one of our first dates, we went to see "The Sound of Music," which premiered in 1965, the movie an immersive experience in Cinerama. When we exited the theatre, Cliff threw leftover popcorn into the air, pretending it to be snow. "Whee!" he shouted into the brisk air of the theatre parking lot. "Look at it snow. And more to come!" flinging another fistful into the air. I felt embarrassed because he was so loud, and also because movie-going was forbidden to Mennonites in those days. Trying to shush him then was impossible, and now I wouldn't even care to try.

Humor was built into Cliff's performances too. His shows, especially the History of Art productions, featured Cliff as cartoonist drawing live caricatures of students and teachers. Drawing a likeness of the principal was usually the highlight of the show—the climax, delighting the students. Once a principal, a rather stout one, stood on the platform, trying to be a good sport, smiling slightly as her image in caricature was evolving. Seconds later, Cliff noticed a slight shift in her posture. As he glanced toward the woman, he noticed she was tilting at an odd angle toward the rear-view projection screen and the heavy wooden side panel. Realizing she was starting to faint, he leaped toward the woman, leaning awkwardly in slow motion. He tried to hold her and the collapsing display as she slipped further onto the stage floor, his black primary crayon still in one fist.

Cliff going out entrance-only door in post office during college days

22 – My Husband's Humor

Cliff drawing caricature of a director at the Georgia Rehabilitation Center in Warm Springs, GA

It's true, without straining very hard, we can find humor in the most trying of circumstances. But sometimes we are confounded by how events in our lives turn out, discovering amusement only in retrospect.

My Checkered Life: A Marriage Memoir

Chapter 23

My Marriage in Vacuum Cleaners

Until the day she died, my mom still had the same vacuum cleaner she'd used for decades: a blue, bullet-shaped machine with a snorkel hose at one end. Think of a mechanical Dachshund, a hot dog with a waist-line problem. Though an ancient model, "It still does the job," she would say, when I took out the vacuum cleaner and helped her clean and fluff up the carpeting in the bedrooms upstairs.

As a couple, we are not quite as frugal or married to a brand as Mom though. As newlyweds, Cliff and I bought a Filter Queen, a squatty brown thing that rolled along the floor on four tiny wheels, a vacuum cleaner that came with a great sales pitch: It could suck up marbles and had a Hepa Filter, a pleated mechanical air filter which removed dust, pollen, mold, and bacteria from the air. Picture the cone-shaped spaceship that returns from outer space, splashing down in the ocean: that's the Hepa filter. The salesman also said it was clean enough to use on a submarine. Cliff experimented with the suck-up marble trick, but I'm sure he never tried it on a submarine.

A few years ago, I was getting tired of my upright Kenmore vacuum, sick and tired of its spewing out more dust than it sucked in. Usually, we employ due diligence researching a good replacement, but Cliff was out of town on his spring tour, so I thought, I can handle this myself . . . how hard can it be? A woman with a mission, I went to Linens and Things, a chain store now defunct in Jacksonville, where I intended to check out my options. I totally breezed by mainstays like Hoover and Electrolux sitting snugly side by side.

Then I spotted a vacuum cleaner at 70 percent off, part of a going-out-of-business sale. Overlooking its heft, I compared it to a cleaner parked close by in the showroom, a Dyson brand, my gold-standard at the time. This model would be perfect, sturdy and top of the line, I thought.

When Husband came home, he just stared at my purchase open-mouthed and started laughing "heh-heh," and then a wild guffaw. His comments: "This thing looks like it can suck up the rug in one fell swoop. Why, it could even pull a red wagon with a child sitting in it around the block–a vacuum cleaner on steroids. That's what it is. A turbo-charged Bissell beast!"

23 – My Marriage in Vacuum Cleaners

To Reflect

Has your mate or someone else in your household ever brought home an item that seemed inappropriate—or even outrageous?

My Checkered Life: A Marriage Memoir

Chapter 24

Explosion in the Curio Cabinet

Besides conniptions with a vacuum cleaner, we've experienced more excitement within the walls of our house. Just ask the curio cabinet. It's still standing in the corner of our dining room. But one evening, it survived internal combustion, an explosion of fireworks.

It was twilight. And twilight was turning to dusk as Cliff and I sat down to eat supper.

He said, "Let's light a candle."

She said, "Well, that's a good idea. It'll look pretty!"

One of us said, "Let's put the candle into the curio cabinet. The mirrors behind will amplify the light."

"Okay," said the other. And so, we admired the ambient light illuminating the cups and curios. "It would look even prettier if we closed the glass door. More shimmer and glisten."

Just so you know: We have surrounded a lighted candle with irreplaceable china. The deceptively romantic light disguised the fact that the candle flame was heating the upper glass shelf! We left the dining room momentarily to clear the table.

BOOM, BANG, POW—The glass shelf shatters. Shards of glass cascade into the once placid display of nineteen antique cups, some from Grandma Longenecker, some from Mother, and some from Cliff's travels to towns with antique shops.

I scream with the first Boom. Then I scream louder as I survey the damage. Cups with dismembered handles. Saucers in slices. Family heirlooms gone with a poof.

24 – Explosion in the Curio Cabinet

Grandma Longenecker's tea cup decorated with green apples, the design arranged in a spray of blossoms with a ladybug and butterflies—gone! The saucer sat in pieces too. Another cup I inherited from Grandma, the turquoise one she used to explain her version of tasseography—in splinters. I was thankful Mother's tiny teacup and saucer set, the one edged in royal blue with feminine figures clad in red—intact. "This is very valuable," she told me when she gifted me with the Japanese demitasse set. Fortunately, our teacups from Buckingham Palace were spared, thank God! Small miracles, but miracles nonetheless.

Indeed, Cliff and I have shared many meals together, but none more explosive than this one.

Fortunately a Japanese teacup from Grandma Annie Metzler survived the explosion

24 – Explosion in the Curio Cabinet

Just because a scene looks alluring doesn't mean it's not dangerous. And, just because a candle is seated in a pretty place doesn't mean the laws of combustion won't operate.

To Reflect

Have you experienced the loss of family heirlooms?

Other distressing material losses?

Have you instigated a clever idea that turned out to be disastrous?

My Checkered Life: A Marriage Memoir

Chapter 25

Conehead Confession

Mouth agape, wide-eyed and stunned at the WaWa gas station in suburban Jacksonville, Florida, I beheld a tee-shirted man holding a frosty drink and belly laughing at me. In the bay just ahead, this guy observed what I failed to see: two traffic cones smashed under my two wheels, front and back. Not one, but two—smashed flat!

Seconds earlier I had felt a ripple on my driver's side tire but my car moved ahead, haltingly. Yes, I had detected some resistance but thought it may have been the metal caps of an underground well for holding gas. No, sireee!

Then I heard a disembodied voice over the service station intercom announcing for all to hear, "Ma'am, you've just run over two traffic cones. This pump is out of order. Move ahead to the next one."

The Frostee-drinking guy took his sweet time to mount his truck, pull on his seat belt and move ahead, but when I cleared the out-of-order pump and moved on to where he had been gassing up, I turned back to see one of the lurid orange cones re-inflate halfway, the other still flat. As I pushed the nozzle into my gas tank though, both smashed orange cones stood straight up. That blessed image caught my full attention.

I could safely remove my dunce cap.

The Cause

I had just come from a riotous lunch with friends at J. Alexander's restaurant. No alcohol, just endorphins from laughter with friends, or so I imagine now.

25 – Conehead Confession

How could this have happened? Spotting the station, I had approached what looked like an available pump, maneuvering my steering wheel hard left, a tight hook to line up to the screen and nozzles of the gas pump I was aiming for.

No out-of-order sign appeared in my line of vision. No obvious orange cones either, a giveaway for an out-of-service pump. Maybe my crossover, a high-off-the-ground vehicle, obstructed my view.

Still, why, oh, why did I do such a dumb thing? I guess I forgot to take my Smart Pill!

I felt a surge of gratitude for flexible, reinflatable traffic cones! In retrospect, I guess I was trying to re-enact a scene in *Coneheads*, the movie starring Jane Curtin and Dan Aykroyd.

Cliff didn't think my mistake was that big of a deal. He could understand that the cones had been placed too close to the pump to be visible as I turned into the bay. He was amused at how embarrassed I felt over what he would consider a rather trivial incident. Still, he enjoyed my animated re-telling of my true story.

To Reflect

It's your turn to tell your "accidental" story. Maybe, like mine, embarrassment is part of the tale.

My Checkered Life: A Marriage Memoir

Chapter 26

Where's My Spyglass?

The photo of a pair of "transitions" eye glasses attached to a scarlet lanyard is still posted on my archived Facebook page dated April 14, 2016. The caption read, "Hubby makes a lanyard for my glasses today. He is not just being kind. He simply doesn't want me to solicit his help to look for my glasses anymore!... well, yes, he is being kind."

I've always been absent-minded, but aging hasn't improved my proclivity to lose items like keys, important documents, and, yes, eyeglasses. Cision, the PR newswire reports that the average American spends about 2.5 days each year looking for lost items. After I posted the photo of the lanyard on social media, comments came from sympathizers and a naysayer: "Funny that I got a store-bought one in my Christmas stocking." Another stated, "Doesn't look very practical. I predict you don't use it much." Yet another commented, "I can absolutely relate!"

My Checkered Life: A Marriage Memoir

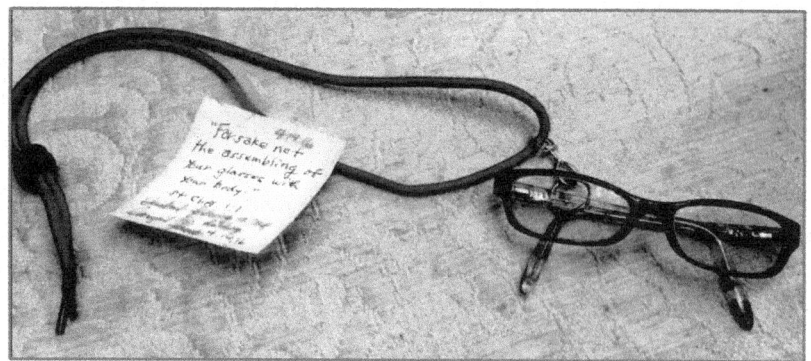

Reading over my Facebook heading again now, I sense myself thinking at the time, "I won't lose my glasses again." A trace of boastfulness? Perhaps. Presumption? Probably so.

Here's how the glasses story subsequently unfolded: On Friday, April 29, 2016, I went to my power-pump class at the gym. Obviously, I wore glasses to drive there and back. I'm nearsighted and a threat on the highway without them. Why, without glasses I might crash.

That evening, we saw a scary Netflix movie, a British Gothic flick *The Making of a Lady*. I must have worn my glasses then. I don't remember squinting or sitting up close, cross-legged, to see the screen. I also don't remember whether my lanyard was around my neck.

The next morning, I planned to drive to grandson Curtis' soccer game at 8:30 a.m. At 8:10 I grabbed my keys and my glasses. My g – g – g l a s s s e e s s s. *Where are they?*

26 – Where's My Spyglass?

Too embarrassed to ask Cliff for help right away, I scoured the usual places: My computer desk, my dresser, the coffee table, the kitchen counter. I couldn't even find my back-up pair usually sitting snugly in the console by the driver's seat.

Then, I go into full-out search mode. With and without Mr. Red Lanyard Maker, I follow a sequence:

1. Look on every surface without a flashlight.
2. Check every surface *with* a flashlight, lifting seat cushions.
3. Walk outside and check the patio furniture, flower-bed containers.
4. Re-visit the front porch table.

Repeat steps 1 and 2 at night. With different lighting, I hoped I'd catch a gleam of glass with my flashlight, after *five hours* of searching, all told.

I awoke with a jolt at 2:00 a.m. with the strong image that my glasses had fallen off my lanyard and into a garbage bag. Then I cull through two plastic bags of trash to no avail.

I prayed ardently. After all, I do remember the story of the Woman with the Lost Coin in the New Testament. In Luke 15, a woman who lost one of her pieces of silver, lit a candle, swept the house, found it, and called her friends together to celebrate. I was ready for celebration!

Catholics would appeal to Saint Anthony, the patron saint of lost items. One online source printed a prayer: "Saint Anthony, Saint Anthony, please come around: Something is lost and needs to be found!" A woman named Madeleine suggested that one call off the hunt as a sign of faith, claiming that "once you say the prayer stop looking for whatever it is you lost."

Well, I did call off the hunt on Sunday, yet kept an eye out. There is always a chance for a miracle. Maybe those two shiny lenses would spontaneously appear.

Apparently, I am not alone. Hunting for lost or misplaced items is common. I have read that the average person spends one year of life looking for keys, wallet — glasses. Among the more distressing losses are diamond rings (Oh, I lost one of those too!)

26 – Where's My Spyglass?

Websites about lost items are usually accompanied by blatant suggestions to get more organized or be more mindful going about one's daily tasks.

Sunday afternoon, the highly-motivated Red Lanyard Maker drove me to Lens Crafters to fix the problem. After all, Mr. RLM can't be my chauffeur for the foreseeable future.

At the optometrist's office, I got an eye examination, another prescription, and new glasses with identical frames, promised in a fortnight.

As I write now, my lanyard is securely hugging my neck with glasses attached. More mindful? Yes, I believe so.

To this day, I haven't found my glasses. Nor have the back-up pair appeared either. Had some genie or sprite spirited away both sets of glasses? Odd and distressing! If the originals make their appearance, I'll be thrilled to use them as my spare.

Wearing my eyeglass lanyard is an off and on proposition for me. Sad to say, I get distracted and forget to don the red lanyard as part of my morning routine. However, one May morning many years later, I was wearing my glasses, an updated prescription but with similar frames. I am proud to say they were securely fastened on the tiny metal loop dangling from the lanyard. But then they disappeared. Vanished! Spirited off into the Land of Lost Lenses!

My Checkered Life: A Marriage Memoir

My mind is clear in the morning. Usually. Now another search is on. Once again, the similar scenario: Check on the usual spots with the naked eye. Then retrace my steps with a flashlight, hoping desperately for a glassy gleam to reflect back to me. Ten minutes in, I reluctantly summon my sidekick. Embarrassed again, of course. At long last, Cliff and I call off the search, and I dig out my spare, a backup pair, the one with transition lenses but a weaker prescription. They'll have to do until I find my best pair.

Then later, several days later in fact: "What's this I see?" My husband had been rooting around in our fridge's freezer section to find his emergency stash of Chic-Fil-A coffee, frozen in case he runs out of his fresh supply. To un-earth it, he has to move aside other products, including a large pouch of Tilapia fish. Not believing his eyes, he notices an odd object–frosted lenses with one wine-colored arm barely visible.

Cliff brings them into the bedroom and presents them to me on an antique saucer. "This looks like something you have been looking for!" He had pulled out my super-cold glasses, frozen at zero degrees Fahrenheit. Yes, frozen, but intact.

"Unbelievable!" I exclaim, snapping a photo of my spectacles, alien in such an environment. Pulling out my visual friend by its arm (aka temple), I gently lay it down on the granite countertop to warm up to room temperature.

"How did this *happen*?" was the first question out of my mouth.

26 – Where's My Spyglass?

Apparently, the arm on one side of my glasses, slid out of the round, metal loop of my lanyard as I stooped to open the freezer door. And it nestled, perhaps with the smallest of sounds, under the pouch of fish. My visual "buddies" had lain there, slowly freezing, as I dashed around the house, looking, in a feverish frenzy.

I think of cliches, some with variation: "Hidden in [not-so-plain] sight."

"An ounce of prevention is worth a pound of cure."

But what if the prevention—and the cure—cancel out each other? Then what?

From my experience, our possessions seem to disappear in direct proportion to their degree of importance in our lives.

To Reflect

Have you found a lost item in a strange place or made a miraculous discovery?

Whether you use eyeglasses or not, do you observe the world with bifocals, seeing the needs of others, close at hand, or at a distance?

My Checkered Life: A Marriage Memoir

Chapter 27

Lunatic in London

As soon as the wedding bells stopped tolling when our son Joel married Sarah, we made big plans to tour Europe. Cliff's Delta Sky Miles had accrued thousands of points, because of his flying home weekends from doing multimedia art shows. Points equated to dollars. We could use points instead of dollars to fund our flights. In 1996, the year our youngest child left home, Cliff had been doing shows for over twelve years, creating and booking his own performances under the aegis of American Art Assemblies. In those days, SkyMiles could expire, so we had to take advantage of the window of opportunity while Delta points were still valid. Besides, we felt a pause in our parenting. Both our daughter Crista and son Joel had made it through four years of college, and both had found suitable mates. We celebrated their weddings. Our children had flown from the nest. Why, we were empty nesters. Now it was our time to fly! London, Rome, Paris... here we come.

I knew we were in trouble when the rotary route took us around Buckingham Palace and not directly to the Comfort Inn, Hyde Park, where we were aiming to roost for the night. Never mind that the steering wheel on our dark blue Vauxhall was set to the right, opposite the American style. Or that Cliff drove on the left side of the road in order to turn right. Or that I as volunteer navigator gripped the creased paper touring map of London, my head bobbing up and down trying to match street signs with landmarks, occasionally screaming to direct the driver.

In mid-August of 1996, we were not exactly neophytes to travel out of the country. After all, we'd been to Montreal, Banff, and Jasper in Canada. Why, England should be a snap. They speak English there too. Besides, I love the British accent.

27 – Lunatic in London

We got some rest that evening and were up the next morning eager to explore London. After breakfast, the concierge at the hotel recommended a nice place to get some lunch. We finally found a car park close to our hotel before having lunch at the Swan Pub, which the concierge at our hotel recommended because it was close by. The brochure displayed a cool-looking interior with damask draperies and upholstered mahogany banquettes, offering a refreshing respite for our tired bodies on a warm day.

Now we had to figure out whether there was a parking time limit. It looked like a two-hour time limit parking zone, plenty of time for lunch. So, we got a sticker for one hour from the kiosk and affixed it to the windshield as directed. Mind you, we paid in British pounds sterling (clinky-clanky coins – not paper currency) so we heard the payment registering in the kiosk. Just like in a slot machine.

Lunch was taking longer than we expected, so I leaped over to the car park to buy another windshield sticker to extend our parking time. Of course, we wouldn't want to get ticketed on our first full day in London. How humiliating that would be. And what a hassle!

On our return, we were relieved to see that there was no parking violation displayed on the windshield. But we looked a second time, and "Oh, no," we groaned, "there IS a suspicious piece of paper hidden under one of the windshield wipers!" I then sprang into action and yelled to Cliff, "This must have just happened. I'm going to track down the patrolman who gave us the ticket!"

My Checkered Life: A Marriage Memoir

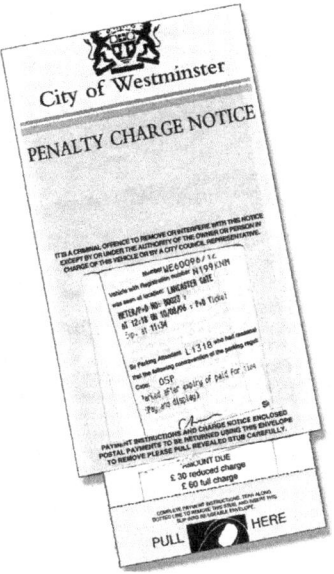

Galloping down the sidewalk with citation in hand, I spied a London parking warden who looked as though he could be on patrol.

"Sir, (trying to hold my emotions in check) you gave us this parking violation ticket, but we have paid for two hours of parking, sufficient for the time used." I urged him to check our windshield and he graciously complied, walking back to the car with me.

With careful scrutiny, he replied, "I realize, Ma'am, that you paid the full amount, but the total parking time has to be reflected on one sticker, not two, even though the amount you paid was sufficient."

"Well, that makes no sense at all," I retorted. "We have paid the City of Westminster/London the full amount, why should it matter how many stickers are displayed on the car?"

Unruffled, the gentle warden restated his case, emphasizing once again the city's policy. Now I shifted into a higher gear of ire. "Well, I am shocked that you don't recognize that you have received payment in full. This isn't right. I want to speak to your supervisor," I insisted.

27 – Lunatic in London

Reasonable, the officer made an effort to accommodate me. He spoke with a measured beat. "I can call him, but you'll have to wait. He's not available right now."

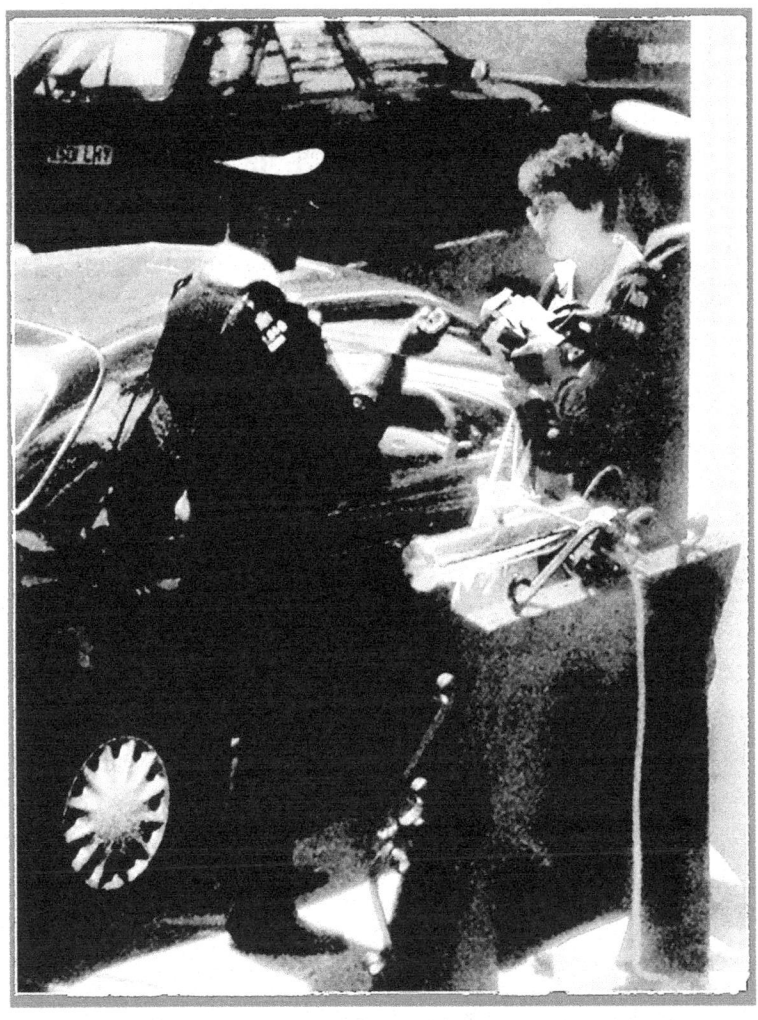

"Fine! I'll wait for as long as it takes," I retorted, now more determined than ever to press my case. With this assurance, Cliff and I drove back to the street by our hotel, awaiting justice. Obligingly, the officer followed us to the hotel. Soon I saw two parking patrol wardens both in black jackets, official hats, and shiny badges heading toward me.

By now, husband Cliff, usually the confrontational one, had ambled slowly toward our room in the hotel. Oh, so I see he's not getting involved in this brouhaha. In fact, the next time I saw my husband was out of the corner of my eye as he was filming the spectacle from the second floor of our hotel while I shouted at the officer and his supervisor on the street below.

27 – Lunatic in London

Determined, I stated my case again to both. I was going to make sure that Mr. Bobby Supervisor saw my point of view. "I want you to rescind this ticket. The City of Westminster has gotten more than enough pounds for the time our car was parked. It is unjust to give us this citation when we have done nothing wrong."

And so it went:

They: But you...

Me: But we...

At one point I was aware of being out of control but felt powerless to stop myself. So, like a crazy woman, I dug myself in deeper.

Apparently, the officers had met irate travelers before and to be conciliatory, they concluded that "By the time your case comes up in court, you will be gone." *Were they going to shoot us?*

Happily, we escaped other consequences from the ticket even though the Vauxhall was a rental car, and the company could have insisted on payment for parking when we got home to the States.

Moral of the story: When jet lag and culture shock collide, watch out for an explosion!

My Checkered Life: A Marriage Memoir

27 – Lunatic in London

To Reflect

Can you relate to an experience like this one?

Do you have a tale of your own to tell?

Chapter 28

Meet Me Under the Bougainvillea

On another trip abroad, the clash of cultures occurred between Cliff and me, not with the *carbinieri,* or *polizia,* when we visited Italy a few years later in 1999. We were vacationing along the southern coast of the boot-shaped country, enjoying the ambiance of the Amalfi coast, a more relaxing pace than we had experienced earlier in Rome.

Quaint Positano, a terraced town poised on a peninsula along the coast on a vertiginous slope to the sea rises up, up, up to houses crouched in cozy rows and leans down, down, down to the snug little village below. We have left the charming hotel, Villa Rosa, to check out the sights and go shopping. Positano itself is dripping with bellissimo: lemons the size of grapefruit, grapes a million, shiny red peppers, elegant shoppes, delikatessens, the Italian word for shops offering cooked cold meats, cheese, and salads for a quick meal. Cliff wanted to check out the sights first and I preferred the shopping, so we decided to meet at a certain time and place "under the bougainvillea" after we went our separate ways.

A host of pergolas of bougainvillea adorned the village, each pergola with blooms that cascaded like crimson waterfalls. I think: *He must mean the one on the way down the steep street leading into the village.*

*Bougainvilleas beside the Church of
Santa Maria Assunta*

28 – Meet Me Under the Bougainvillea

In one of the shops, plates of lemon yellow and Mediterranean blue caught my eye, imprinted with authentic painting on the back "dipinto a mano per alimenti Positano"–a hand-painted dish. They came bubble-wrapped so I could snuggle them against breakage between layers of clothing in my suitcase. I couldn't decide between the blue and the yellow, so I got two of each, complementary in color for a table setting.

Soon it would be noon, the time we agreed to meet before lunch. I left the shops and meandered back up to the brilliant bougainvillea to people-watch and wait for my prince. I waited and waited. No Cliff in sight! That's just like him, losing track of time when he's snapping photos, I thought. The minutes pass and I'm starting to get mad. The temperature on my "mad"

gauge rises even higher as the sun beat down furiously on my head. "Why didn't I wear a straw hat? Where is that man?"

Mad turns slowly to sad as I realized he must have fallen over from heat exhaustion and lay at the foot of the Duomo, his camera case splayed beside his prostrate body. "Oh, my goodness, do they have ambulances in such a small town?" I hadn't heard sirens here, unlike Rome where horns hee-haw all hours like electronic donkeys. Finally, I convinced myself Cliff wasn't dead and probably still wandering around. My emotions cycled between mad and sad a few more times until I saw a tall, blond man approaching me looking very mad himself, certainly not glad to see me again.

C. "Where have you been? I've been waiting for you by the bougainvillea for more than an hour now!"

M. "Well, I could ask the same thing. I have been waiting ages under this pergola for you. I thought you might have keeled over from the heat. Where in the world were you?"

C. "Don't you remember? The last thing we talked about was the bougainvillea by the Duomo, so I thought that was the place we were supposed to meet!"

In 1999, we didn't have cellphones, though we noticed many Italians did, especially in large cities like Rome. With electronic connection at our disposal, this blow-up would probably have never happened.

28 – Meet Me Under the Bougainvillea

We rehearsed the scenario far too long and tried to resolve the mix-up by arguing our own points of view, an exercise in futility. What we did agree on is a cool place for lunch which for us was a tomato-drenched pasta (larvae-shaped noodles) entrée and an omelet. I exchanged a pile of eggplant "aubergine" for an "ensalada mista," garden salad.

Bellissimo!

Pergola with bougainvillea by the road leading up to the Villa Rosa Bed & Breakfast

To Reflect

I'll bet you have a story similar to this one but probably with a different setting. Tell your story to someone else, maybe someone of another generation.

My Checkered Life: A Marriage Memoir

Chapter 29

Slights and Offenses: How Do You Handle Them?

Story 1: Tree Falls on Roof

Snafus and misunderstandings can happen much closer to home. We can get hurt in our day-to-day interactions with others. Often our elevated expectations of how other people behave can lead to disappointment or disillusionment. And truth be told, we can even feel upset when the conflict happens within ourselves. The two stories that follow illustrate both aspects of the misunderstanding conundrum.

"Uh, oh, look here." Cliff was perusing local news online in our city newspaper. "Here's a photo of Kitty and Karl Ellison's house. A big, old live oak fell on their roof yesterday!" I shivered as I glanced at the disturbing sight. Seconds later, I felt a different emotion. Though the nasty news made me feel sorry for the Ellisons, who had just remodeled their home, it also dredged up a grudge I had held against Kitty for over a year now.

Earlier, Kitty was in a position to weigh in on the decision to have Cliff present one of his art & music programs to an organization she was part of. She nixed the idea at a time when the booking would have been most welcome. Ever since, when I saw her in social settings, I felt the sting of the offense. Whatever the excuse may have been: "No money in the budget"... "We don't want to ask attendees for a donation"... had sounded lame to me. In short, her decision registered in my heart and mind like a sharp jab.

But a tree had fallen on their house! The horrible event could have made me think, "Serves her right," she is not a charitable person anyway. But instead, I felt sympathy. A few years earlier, a tree had fallen neatly *beside* our house, with very little damage done. From the looks of things, the Ellisons would have to move out of their house now, live in a hotel for a while, and petition the insurance company to cover the huge damages. Now it was my turn for an "Uh, oh!"

29 – Slights and Offenses: How Do You Handle Them?

My "Uh, oh" was followed by a change of heart. Instead of feeling secretly happy at the Ellisons' bad luck, I wrote a check and sent it to them with a note. It wasn't a large check, but it was an acknowledgment of my empathizing with their situation. As the envelope with the check sailed off through the mail, I felt relief, a huge burden of bitterness lifted. Sending the check broke the power the spirit of unforgiveness had wielded over me. In return, Kitty sent me a Thank You note, which I've held onto for years as a reminder to forgive, to let go of bitterness.

The thank-you note sent to me by Kitty

In retrospect, I am certain the slight I felt was not intentional. And I probably shouldn't have taken Kitty's decision personally.

What others say or do often has nothing at all to do with us.

Sometimes their behavior mirrors their own interior struggles. Perhaps their response to us is a reaction to something else going on in their lives completely unrelated to us. In the end, my antagonism was replaced with empathy, a feeling I could peaceably live with.

The names and certain details have been changed

"To forgive is to set a prisoner free and discover that the prisoner was me."
– Lewis B. Smedes

"Love your enemies! Do good to them. . . . Then your reward from heaven will be very great, and you will truly be acting as sons of God: for he is kind to the unthankful and to those who are very wicked."
– Luke 6:35, *The Living Bible*

To Reflect

Can you identify in any way with my story?

How do you handle slights and offenses?

29 – Slights and Offenses: How Do You Handle Them?

Story 2: Crying, A Slice in Time

I have been blogging since 2013 and over time, I felt energized creating posts and then joining the conversation with readers who respond to my posts with their comments: "Yes, I can relate!" or "Have you thought of this?"

Stories about my early Mennonite life especially resonated with readers. They wanted more of these from me. And so, in 2015, I began entertaining the idea of using my blog stories to create scenes in a memoir. An academic, trained in analytical thinking, I had no idea how to tell a story well on paper, much less organize a group of stories into a book. I took a course in memoir writing from Linda Joy Myers and Brooke Warner, who taught me how to identify turning points in my life, which could help develop a narrative arc readers could follow.

Then, I enrolled in a family history course from author/poet Ben Vogt, who gave me clues about how to be specific in my description. He too was teacherly, always affirming. But he was also incisive, biting into the scripts I send him with loud barks in return, some comments in caps: HOW BIG IS MEDIUM? YOU'VE GOT TO BE FAR MORE DETAILED AND DESCRIPTIVE FOR US.

To be fair, every once in a while, I saw that I have succeeded: "GREAT PARAGRAPH!" he shouted once in all caps. He was thrilled when I used sensory detail (All five senses now!) to properly develop a scene instead of resorting to flabby adjectives. Then I was both surprised–and pleased.

When I thought the manuscript was as good as I could make it, I gave it to several blog readers in 2018. Authors themselves, they gave me great feedback, letting me know when my prose sang, or when my thoughts were murky. Then I hired two developmental editors to assess the manuscript for structure and clarity. Copyediting and proofreading followed, and then in August 2019, I received early print editions of *Mennonite Daughter: The Story of a Plain Girl.* Oh, happy day!

29 – Slights and Offenses: How Do You Handle Them?

I'm not a public figure, nor am I a celebrity, but my memoir was well received with healthy sales, especially as the book launched. I was especially heartened when a reviewer told me, reading about my path toward forgiveness of my father's heavy-handedness, "This happened to me too. I can relate." Or, from another, "I love how you describe walking in your Grandma's woods. I felt as though I was actually *there*."

In 2021 as I continued blogging, I felt the urge to explore other topics in a book. I tossed these questions around in my head: "Should I organize Aunt Ruthie's diaries into a book? What about my life after I left Pennsylvania and got married? Would readers be interested in that?" At the time, no clear answers about how to proceed emerged. I felt stymied.

One morning in September 2021, I took one of our twice weekly walks with my neighbor Barbara. And this is what spilled out, a vignette with the simple title "Crying."

I've been wanting to cry for days now. Not because of anything specific, just general malaise from following the prickly path of my life as a writer: feeling stuck in my next project, seeing just a trickle of monetary results from my first book, two and a half years out. Feeling like it was all too much. I tried to cry, believing it would open clogged channels and relieve stress.

This morning, I prepared for the day, slathering moisturizer with sunscreen on my face, knowing I would walk with my neighbor Barbara in the bright Florida morning. "Walking will loosen my stiff joints," she said.

"I definitely agree," I replied, even though I was concentrating on my right eye, which was beginning to sting. Why was that? Apparently, the lotion I'd put on my face with a SPF of 35 had oozed into my eye as the heat and humidity increased during our walk.

As I sat down in my writing studio, the irritation worsened. *Okay, I'll press a wet washcloth to my eyelid.* The pain became even worse. Then, I dropped some eye solution onto my cornea. It didn't help much. More eye drops, a soaped-up washcloth. Then, I turned my face under the faucet and let the flow irrigate my eye. That helped a little, but then my nose started to run.

Finally, I began to cry, clearing out sinuses and all the emotion stuck behind my eyes and lodged in my heart.

"Her [Kay's] throat felt thick inside; it was the lump that forms when it might help to cry but tears don't come."
– Amy Kenyon in *Ford Road*

"Praise be to the God and Father of our Lord Jesus Christ, the Father of compassion and the God of all comfort, who comforts us in all our troubles, so that we can comfort those in any trouble with the comfort we ourselves receive from God."
– II Corinthians 1:3-4, *New International Version*

To Reflect

How have you tried to vent your emotions when you feel stressed?

29 – Slights and Offenses: How Do You Handle Them?

My Checkered Life: A Marriage Memoir

Chapter 30

Flash in the Pan: A Sunday Morning Argument

Snafus and misunderstandings that deliver the hardest punches are those with a mate. It could also happen with another partner in your household. This one occurred just as the cloud of the corona virus began to invade the atmosphere of our home in March of 2020.

When the COVID pandemic hit our country early in 2020, we had been married nearly 53 years. With so many years together, we had experienced sickness and health, the better and the worse. But nothing prepared us (or anyone else) for the isolation from normal activities and being quarantined would bring. For families, the separation was coupled with extreme togetherness. As a matter of fact, Cliff and I clashed on a Sunday morning, just three days after our city had announced a complete shutdown.

My Checkered Life: A Marriage Memoir

Five large eggs sat happily agitating in the boiling water on my shiny black, glass stovetop. It was Sunday morning, the first Sunday of our state's shutdown due to the COVID-19 pandemic. It felt odd not preparing to go to church to teach my 2-year-old preschoolers and attend the worship service that followed with Cliff.

Nevertheless, I was determined to make the best of it. Why not make a hot breakfast for Cliff? Surely, I had the time. Already, eggs being hard-boiled for later pickling in brine had begun to boil. While the water was still piping hot, I figured I could surprise my husband.

"How about I make you a soft-boiled egg? It'll be simple to add another egg to the pot."

"Well, okay, that would be nice." Freshened and shaved, my husband smiled weakly as he ambled into the kitchen, expecting to prepare his usual breakfast of cereal and fruit.

30 – Flash in the Pan: A Sunday Morning Argument

I plopped the fresh egg into the water–one just for him.

"It'll be done in a little over three minutes," I chirped. "Watch the clock. It'll be 8:42 when the egg can come out." As Cliff waited and watched, he popped a slice of fresh sourdough bread into the toaster.

Walking into the bedroom close by to put on my robe, I could hear the egg skittering around on the plate as he spooned it from the pot, just in the nick of time. As I arrived back in the kitchen, he was assembling a napkin, fork and butter knife to crack the egg. After putting his steaming cup of coffee on the bamboo tray, he shuffled away into his studio to eat breakfast. I'm a morning person, fired up to greet the day; Cliff takes longer to waken and show signs of alertness. Still, I could tell he appreciated the gesture, especially unexpected on a day when the whole world had suddenly stopped.

I could picture my husband enjoying his egg breakfast, the bright sun slanting in from the east, cheering his corner studio. Four years ago, when we transitioned to this house in suburban Jacksonville, I visualized how Cliff could create more art work in this space, like the painting of five swans swimming in a lake under a big rainbow, an image at odds with the blow-up in the kitchen that I didn't know was about to erupt in our usually happy household.

Back in the kitchen, I met Cliff with his empty tray. Wearing a broad smile, I knew I had done something special for him at the start of a strange day. "How was the egg?" I asked jubilantly.

"Well, it tasted fine, but it wasn't quite done," he muttered.

Disappointed and deflated, in a flash I could picture the yellow-orange egg dripping over the toast, the white of the egg still in its puberty. I could imagine my husband twirling the knife around the inside of the shell, releasing the clear, gelatinous egg white. I had failed! This was proof! Instantly, I flipped from mild disappointment to full-on anger.

"You always criticize me!" I yelled menacingly. With that, I stomped, militantly, to our bedroom, slamming the door.

The global ghost, the coronavirus pandemic, had just gripped our nation and the world. Whisperings that had begun in China, and then spread to Italy were beginning to create waves of terror in our own country. As I recall my blow-up, I realize now that the invasion of the virus into our lives may have triggered the stages of grief, at least for me as stated in the Kubler-Ross model: denial, anger, bargaining, depression and finally, acceptance.

And it had occurred to me that I had probably hit Stage 2, anger, just a few days after the crisis had registered in my psyche. With churches and stores closed and our city at a standstill in mid-March 2020, denial was not an option for me.

Though the emotional temperature in the house had plumeted to near freezing, in the bedroom, I stewed, "I must have lit a firecracker." Feeling offended by Cliff's negative reaction but also instantly angry at my short fuse, I remained in the bedroom to nurse my hurt feelings.

30 – Flash in the Pan: A Sunday Morning Argument

"What will happen next?" I wondered, after I had time to gather my thoughts. As long-marrieds, we rarely argue anymore. I try to avoid fights because they require so much energy. But when they happen, Cliff is more eager to make up than I am. Sitting on the edge of the bed, I realized I had over-reacted, but I was in no mood to make amends just yet. I wanted to stay mad a while longer. And so, I bided my time in the bedroom. Too irritated to confront my husband right away, I pondered, "Who will make the first move?"

After several minutes of brooding, I ventured back into the kitchen. There was my husband, possibly trying a different tack to restore harmony.

Cliff was grinning near the counter, a non-stick pan in his hand. He had grabbed two steak knives, facing them in opposing directions. Apparently, he had raided cosmetics on my vanity too: Between the two knives was a tube of lipstick, its scarlet cylinder swiveled open. "Here, if we're going to have a duel, you pick the weapon!"

I stood uncomprehendingly at first, blinking at this odd display of two knives and a lipstick in the pan. And then I got it: *Duel or duet?* The tension eased, Cliff laughed and I laughed too. Holding the pan with one hand, he pulled me toward him with the other hand, and we hugged.

"Clever idea. Clever," I said, smiling with relief.

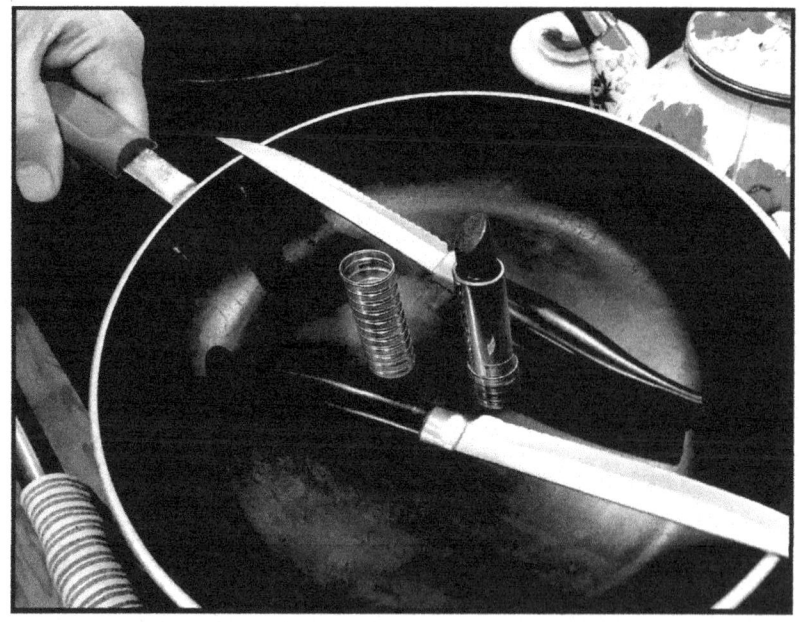

Our "flash in the pan" was a clash: contentious, but over quickly. It was likely a consequence of my reckoning with the fear of the unknown, which the onset of the coronavirus had injected into our lives, personally and as a nation.

However, as a couple in a long-term marriage, we have learned to recognize signs of discord and look for a remedy as quickly as possible. Like the dictionary of idioms affirms, our tiff was a transient occurrence with no long-term effect. Thank God for a husband who has learned to solve our marital problems in a novel way. Next time, it may be my chance to be the creative "duel diffuser"!

30 – Flash in the Pan: A Sunday Morning Argument

Over decades of give and take, I have learned to keep my mouth shut over trivial matters. Arguing takes a lot of energy. When we go out to eat, choosing a restaurant is more important to Cliff than it is to me, so I often let him choose. But sometimes I spout off. When would that happen? When Cliff changes from outdoor shoes to ones he wears indoors and sometimes unthinkingly takes them off just outside the front door or close to the sliding door to the lanai. Then I stumble because I can't see the shoes when I'm carrying a bag of trash or the recycling box. I confess, that's when I yell, "Why don't you think where you put your shoes when you take them off?"

Actually, there are many opportunities for each of us to get ruffled feathers, but when it's up to me, I make an effort to choose romance over a ruckus.

To Reflect

What is *your* story about conflict?

Your comments about mine?

My Checkered Life: A Marriage Memoir

Chapter 31

Finances: The Mislaid One Hundred Dollars and More

Throughout our marriage, we have put our money into the same pot. No matter who earns the dollars, we share bank accounts and investments. We typically discuss purchases of over two or three-hundred dollars. There are probably other viable ways for other couples to handle finances, but this system works for us. We have always tithed our income, giving at least one-tenth of our income to charity, our church first and then other organizations we think warrant our support.

Over the years, we routinely reserve some of our money for vacations, either to see family or explore new frontiers. In July 2020, when there appeared to be a brief break in the COVID pandemic, we flew to Springfield, Missouri, to visit a second-cousin I'd recently corresponded with via a Facebook connection, Howard Landis. Howard and his wife Faythe had visited our home as they traveled from Missouri to their winter home in Trinity, Florida, so we had had a face-to-face meeting earlier. Now it was our turn to be treated to their hospitality—a cool getaway, a break from sultry summer heat in the South.

I Really Feel Dumb: Cliff Tells His Story

Marian had been in touch with her second cousin Howard for several months now and we were anticipating getting away from the tropical heat and humidity of Jacksonville, Florida, for a few days. We agreed on some mutual dates in July 2021 with Howard and his wife Faythe.

Mennonite Marian had known her second cousin Howard since her childhood. Howard's father was her grandmother's brother's grandson on the Martin side of her family. A second cousin. When Marian was young, occasionally Mary Martin, Howard's mother, came to visit her Aunt Ruthie and Grandmother. Marian felt awed when she saw all the colorful fashions Mary wore. There wasn't a better description of the contrast between Plain and Fancy.

Marian felt cheated to be clothed in simple dresses, a large white covering hiding her beautiful hair all piled up under a prayer cap, according to the rules of Lancaster Mennonite Conference. Marian pondered, "After all, wasn't it God who created beauty and lovely flowers with exciting colors and designs? So why can't I be fancy too?"

We were excited about the trip and had not flown away from Jacksonville since vacationing in British Columbia for our

31 – Finances: The Mislaid One Hundred Dollars and More

50th wedding anniversary four years earlier. COVID restrictions and worries had kept us home.

I was eager to work on airline schedules, hoping to find the best flight connections from Jacksonville to Springfield, Missouri since we were still seven weeks from our departure date. Ticket prices had risen, so we turned to using our Delta frequent flier miles. However, we didn't have enough points for the particular flights and dates I had chosen, so we had to purchase some additional miles. I carefully juggled the itinerary for the best flights, so we would have ample time between connections. I didn't want us having a heart attack running to the gate to make the next flight.

Like usual, I chose some good seats, on the right side, ahead of the wings and noisy engines with a nearby window to peer out of. From a window seat, Marian could enjoy billowy summer clouds and be thankful there was still a green earth outside of the sprawling urban cities. I chose 19F and 19D, with Marian in the adjoining seat when we took off. In my opinion, sitting in the Comfort Plus section was worth the extra money. Flying for thirty years while presenting art and music performances around the country, I noticed the size of the airline seats was getting smaller and the distance between rows was shrinking. Lately I've felt like one of a herd of cattle stuck in a corral with little circles of air above trying to cool me. Every so often I had felt like bellowing out a sorry "Moo."

The departure time for our trip was getting closer. On Saturday, July 9, we drove to Jacksonville Beach where we

My Checkered Life: A Marriage Memoir

were going to attend a celebration of life service at Palms Presbyterian Church for one of Marian's colleagues from Florida State College.

We left a little early and decided we would stop by our credit union to get some cash out for the trip. We mainly use credit cards on trips but in addition have a little cash available for emergencies.

I withdrew $100.00 (two tens and some twenties) and also took out five one-dollar bills to put in Marian's shoebox, used for making change when she sold one of her memoirs when someone paid with cash. I carefully labeled the two white envelopes, one for our trip and one for book change. We still had a little time left to take a short walk on the beach and then proceed to the church. When we got home that afternoon, I sensibly put one of the envelopes on the top of my dresser, the one marked TRIP.

Sunday came and we started packing our suitcases. Finally, I needed to place the cash envelope somewhere safe for the trip. I opened it up and I couldn't believe my eyes. The envelope had only five one-dollar bills in it. What in the world! Who took my traveling money?

I knew that Marian had just made a short trip to the grocery store, so I leaped into the garage and rifled through the empty grocery bags in the back seat of our car. I lifted up anything I could find, checking in every crevice inside the car. Where was it? I really felt dumb.

31 – Finances: The Mislaid One Hundred Dollars and More

Going back into the house, "Honey," I said. "Maybe when you got your groceries it fell out in the parking lot. It would be a miracle if it were still there." The store was just down the street. My heart was racing now. I zoomed to the parking lot and looked far and wide. Nothing. I went home dejected.

For years I had prided myself as being a careful, fastidious planner, trip organizer and had never had this happen. There was no time to get any cash out since we were flying out the next morning. I was feeling dumber.

Our trip to Missouri was great but my goof up reared its head several times in my mind. As soon as we arrived in Springfield, I had to share my story with Howard. He just smiled and didn't think it was a big deal.

Of course, life went on. One day almost one month later on August 19, 2020, I made an amazing find. I was checking through Marian's memoir shoe box for some change and saw a small white envelope with said "$5 Menno D. bag." Curiously I leafed through the envelope and counted out $100.00 in currency.

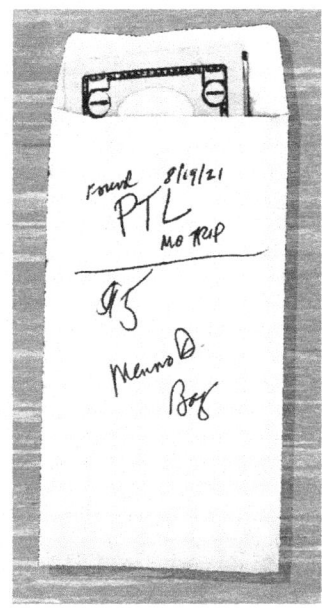

An admonition: Be careful how you label things!

Soon after, I created this card to celebrate finding the missing money.

Wise Solomon admonishes us in Proverbs 23:5, "Wilt thou set thine eyes upon that which is not? For riches certainly make themselves wings; they fly away as an eagle toward heaven."

31 – Finances: The Mislaid One Hundred Dollars and More

Discovering the cash gave Cliff's story a happy ending. And now I'm remembering another story of discovering a bit of cash of my own, a mere dollar bill.

The Story Behind the Dollar Bill

Dollar Discovery! On September 10, 2015, I opened an envelope dated April 30, 1962, a letter that Mother sent me during my junior year at Eastern Mennonite College in Virginia. I had read her letter then, but did not open the Bossler Mennonite Church bulletin until now. There she had tucked a dollar bill (series date 1957). I wonder now whether she was testing to see if I had taken the time to open the bulletin she enclosed. Probably so.

When I opened the bulletin commemorating Church College Day from a few weeks earlier, out tumbled a "Silver Certificate" dollar bill backed by REAL money, not the "Federal Reserve" bills we carry around in our wallets nowadays.

My Checkered Life: A Marriage Memoir

What was going on in the world in April 1962? Among other events, Walter Cronkite replaced Douglas Edwards as anchorman for the CBS evening news. At a London Jazz Club, Brian Jones was introduced to Mick Jagger and Keith Richards of the Rolling Stones, and The World's Fair opened in Seattle, Washington that year.

What was happening in the Longenecker house then?

31 – Finances: The Mislaid One Hundred Dollars and More

Here are excerpts from Mother's letter containing a dollar bill:

"Hello to all the gals at Peachey House.... [An off-campus housing site for upper-class women students] "Did you get your book – – – I mean your 'Books,' The postmaster wants to know if you got the book we sent. Don't forget to tell us. He wants to know how long it took to get to E. M. C."

". . . I called LaVon's mother on Friday. The way it sounds maybe you are taking her place. She is going to work for Dr. Walmer 5 weeks, and then she is going to be counselor at a few camps. She is sure you will like it. She said you even get off the fourth of July with pay. She knows they pay over a dollar an hour but she didn't know right yet how much." [Lavon Nolt Kolb is a school friend: We attended first grade together. Here Mother is discussing summer work for me.]

". . . I started to tell you Janice and I were at the Mother & daughter banquet on Friday eve. They really had a nice program & plenty of food such as fruit cup, a very large slice of ham loaf, baked potato, corn & peas, cold slaw, pickles & olives, celery & carrots, ice cream & cake, mints & nuts. Well, we were just stuffed."

". . . When you get your check get it cashed then you will have what you need."

There are two references to money in this letter posted 1962, three if you count the dollar bill that I didn't discover until

2015. I don't remember what the check was intended for, or the amount, but it was probably not enough for books or tuition. And seldom did Mother write a letter that didn't mention a menu or food preparation.

I know now that she equated food with love. And she knew that money, even a little bit, would sweeten my passage through my college days too.

God bless the memory of my mother who knew the value of a dollar.

To Reflect

When have you overlooked a "hidden" gift, finding it months or years later?

What are your Lost and Found stories?
We all have them. Tell yours.

My Checkered Life: A Marriage Memoir

Part 4

Harmony in Marriage and in Life

"When you are consciously aware of
all that you have to be grateful for,
your life is in perfect harmony."

– Hal Elrod

My Checkered Life: A Marriage Memoir

Chapter 32

Morning Ablution: What's Your Routine?

Here's the true secret of life: We mostly do everything over and over. In the morning, we let the dogs out, make coffee, read the paper, help whoever is around get ready for the day. We do our work. In the afternoon, if we have left, we come home, put down our keys and satchels, let the dogs out, take off constrictive clothing, make a drink or put water on for tea, toast the leftover bit of scone. I love ritual and repetition. Without them, I would be a balloon with a slow leak."

– Anne Lamott, *Stitches: A Handbook of Meaning, Hope, and Repair.*

My own routine is one variation of Lamott's, but a routine nonetheless. If I deviate too far from this ritual, things feel a bit "off." I feel out of kilter. So here's how I counter that:

Step 1: Get up, wash face; dress

Step 2: Make breakfast

Step 3: Time of meditation with Bible & gratitude book.

Step 4: Exercise, walking alone or with a neighbor.

Of course, when I taught college classes, my routine was abbreviated, holding fast to the first three and then grabbing my bookbag by the door and dashing off in my tan Infiniti to the campus four miles away.

Step 5: Begin work

Origin of *ablution*: Late Middle English: from Latin ablutio(n-), from abluere, from ab- 'away' + luere 'wash'. The original use was as a term in chemistry and alchemy meaning "purification by using liquids," hence "purification" of the body by washing' (mid 16th century).

Benefits of Your Routine, according to the "Hello Peaceful Mind" website:

You will...

- Feel less stress
- Gain time
- Be less likely to forget something
- Take better care of yourself
- Eat better in the morning

A *Huffington Post* article adds other benefits including exercise by stretching, taking a shower, and meditation. According to author Julia Cameron, your routine could also include writing morning pages to prime the pump of creativity.

Ben Franklin and Victor Hugo had their own morning routine, reflective of their personalities and habits, which these quotes illustrate.

Early in his life, Benjamin Franklin, one of the primary framers of the American Constitution, outlined his best morning routine:

"...I rise early almost every morning, and sit in my chamber without any clothes whatever, half an hour or an hour, according to the season, either reading or writing."

In Franklin's *Autobiography,* he elaborated he would "rise, wash, and address *Powerful Goodness;* contrive day's business and take the resolution of the day; prosecute the present study; and breakfast."

Victor Hugo, author of *Les Miserables,* awakened by the daily gunshot from the fort near his home, drank a cup of freshly brewed coffee while reading a letter from his mistress, Juliette Drouet, and then swallowed two raw whole eggs.

32 – Morning Ablution: What's Your Routine?

The Power of Habit

"We underestimate the power of habit while we're young, and we underestimate the *grace* of it."

– Jens Christian Grøndahl, *"Often I Am Happy"*

To Reflect

What is your morning routine? Another routine for a different occasion?

What tips can you add to the ones listed here?

My Checkered Life: A Marriage Memoir

Chapter 33

Moving the Body: Finding Balance

My Fitbit is a nosy thing. A bracelet circling my left wrist, this digital device counts my steps during the day. It urges me to reach my daily goal, and its face lights up with fireworks when I reach it. It also knows how to deliver a pulse to my wrist if I've been sitting for too long. The tiny tingle urges me to relieve my neck and shoulders from tension that builds up being hunched over my computer. It also asks if I want to record calories, log sleep, or keep track of menstrual health, laughable—and unnecessary—at this stage of life.

Writing is often a solitary activity, and it's also sedentary. That's why I schedule movement into my day. Since my early forties when I was in the midst of teaching, my gym membership ensured that I'd move my muscles and, along the way, form friendships.

A Pilates class I joined before the COVID pandemic carried me through the lockdown and its social restrictions. Now I still meet via Zoom with friends clad in athletic gear, with our valiant instructor teaching us remotely from her home in North Carolina. In a class of thirty- to fifty-year-olds, I sometimes need to modify the poses, using lighter weights or stretching to my ankles instead of reaching all the way to my feet. I also wear a right knee support and mesh guard on my weak left wrist; I'm not taking any chances. And to tell the truth, I tune in as much to see my friends and our instructor Rachel, Princess of Poses, as I do for the benefits of exercise.

33 – Moving the Body: Finding Balance

What I'm hinting at is self-care, keeping one's body, mind, and spirit in balance. As the years fly by, I realize I have to be intentional, or I'll let good habits slip. Harmony in body and mind doesn't happen accidentally. That's why it's good to have a routine to start the day in reasonably high spirits, to generate enough energy to help you power through the day.

My Checkered Life: A Marriage Memoir

Chapter 34

Lessons from the Bisque Salt and Pepper Shakers

Do you procrastinate? Are there unfinished projects lying about in your house? When we cleared out Aunt Ruthie's house, in the attic, we found a bin of odds and ends with a note attached "Unfinished Projects." Her intention exceeded her life span. We sisters got a laugh out of the tag, I took a photo, but in the end, we tossed the box and contents, a deposit for the dumpster.

Another part of self-care, for me, is being able to tolerate an unfinished task or something else that feels incomplete. And, yet, being willing (when the time is right) to move it toward completion—like sewing a quilt, mending a relationship, or writing a book. Here is a practical lesson from my husband's bisque salt and pepper shakers.

Years ago, in graduate school at Florida State University, Cliff made pale, earth-toned bisque-fired salt and pepper shakers. He said creating the shakers was a side project back then, something he had the urge to do with clay leftover from a major assignment. What is "bisque"? Just so you know, after the clay dries slowly for several days, the initial firing, called a bisque, can be placed into a kiln.

The empty shakers have sat in my china closet for a long time now. For decades, actually. They have a pleasing shape but they are not practical to use on the table without glazing.

Why? Because they are unfinished. In the busy 1970s, Cliff wore several hats including teacher, graduate student, and graphic art business owner. Making the shakers was an impromptu project, a way to use up left-over clay. He wasn't being graded for it.

The need certainly wasn't urgent either. Obviously, I could use other salt and pepper shakers in my kitchen cabinet. So, completing the project with glaze and a final firing fell by the wayside.

Next Steps

According to Cliff, three things would have to happen to make the shakers usable:

1. Use a diamond-tipped drill to finish opening up the holes on top, so each spice could be shaken from the top.

2. Apply a non-toxic glaze followed by a final firing.

3. Insert cork stoppers to the bottom after shaker wells have been filled.

The Lessons

Opportunity still knocks, even though many years have elapsed.

Sometimes one needs to be prodded to take the next step.

It often doesn't take much to finish a job that's partly done.

To Reflect

What unfinished projects await your "next step"?

What would it take to turn them from work-in-progress status to the completion stage?

Have you recently finished a project you're proud of? Do share with someone willing to listen.

34 – Lessons from the Bisque Salt and Pepper Shakers

My Checkered Life: A Marriage Memoir

Chapter 35

Are You Too Big for Your Pot?

"If it isn't one thing, it's another," Mother said, sometimes sighing into thin air, when we were growing up in the Longenecker house, "It's hard to keep up with it all." My mother Ruth made clothes for me, the oldest, which often became hand-me-downs for my sisters. As we grew, she used bigger pots on her stove to accommodate larger appetites, especially with the addition of my brother Mark to the family. Growth always requires adjustments, a fact which a broken pot illustrated one day on my patio at our Killarney Shores house.

I didn't hear a bang. I didn't see the pot fall. But when I looked from the upstairs bedroom window, I saw red chards of pottery on the patio floor. I really liked that shiny red pot and now it lay in pieces. It was a scarlet-red terra cotta pot that contained a wee white orchid and "red sister" plant, an evergreen tropical shrub belonging to the lily family. Thriving in all seasons in northeast Florida, "red sister" has the rather exotic botanical name of "Cordyline Fruticosa."

"How did that happen?" There was no wind. I wasn't aware that a storm had come through during the night. Still the pot had fallen from its perch on the maroon plant stand, three feet above the concrete floor. Encased within the pottery was a plastic inner pot from which roots were dangling. The plant was pot-bound, longing to break free!

35 – Are You Too Big For Your pot

It didn't take a genius to see these tall plants had outgrown their tiny pot, roots bursting through the pot hole.

My solution? Re-pot the plant. Add fertile soil. Use a bigger pot. And then I made the planter pretty too–with an unbreakable, woven basket.

Some of the most memorable lines in Leonard Cohen's "Dance Me to the End of Love" speak of cracks: "Ring the bells that still can ring/Forget your perfect offering/There is a crack, a crack in everything/That's how the light gets in."

I notice at least five lessons here, all applying to the challenges of being human:

- *Even cracks have a function: they let the light in.*

- *You don't have to be perfect to be beautiful. What's broken in you can be a metaphor for human aspiration. Your flaw can produce growth.*

- *When you are pot-bound, move into a bigger pot.*

- *The bigger pot will help the root system to flourish. In order to bloom, the plant needs a source of nutrition, which the thriving roots provide.*

- *While you are mending the mess, observe other flowering plants, "singing" their morning praises.*

King David says, "A broken and a contrite heart thou wilt not despise." - Psalm 51:17

God can restore broken lives and fashion them into something beautiful. That's how we can live harmonious lives, observing a thing of beauty, imagining it to be so, even in its broken condition.

35 – Are You Too Big For Your pot

To Reflect

Think of something broken, a physical object, a relationship, an emotional feeling.

How has it been restored? Or not?

My Checkered Life: A Marriage Memoir

Chapter 36

My Work is Loving The World

Above all else, my work is loving the world, myself included, but also my husband, my family, our neighbors, and all those I contact and can influence.

With hearts of gratitude, we honor the treasures of the land, with its power to heal and its gifts of providing food, clothing, and shelter.

Famed poet Mary Oliver declares that her work is loving the world, especially the natural world.

The land grounds us, provides stability under our feet, nourishes our souls and feeds our bodies. Here as some lines from her poem.

My Work is Loving the World

- *My work is loving the world.*
- *Here the sunflowers, there the hummingbird -- equal seekers of sweetness*
- *Here the quickening yeast; there the blue plums.*
- *Here the clam deep in the speckled sand.*

36 – My Work Is Loving The World

And she continues in her four-stanza poem, expressing joy...

Let me
keep my mind on what matters
which is my work,...
Which is gratitude, to be given a mind and a heart
and these body-clothes,
a mouth with which to give shouts of joy...

- Mary Oliver

Her words inspired me to pay attention to the natural beauty of the sun, the clouds, and the pines in our neighborhood. I express my gratitude and insights through haiku:

The glowing spring sun
Melts over the tops of pine
Spreading like butter

Painted, pink sunrise
Fuels life's bright carousel
Ups, downs, sorrow, joy

Clouds ride north, touch pines
Sun's rays shine downward, content
Never asking why

One summer afternoon, creativity burst forth as I observed a storm:

> *Florida lightning*
> *Falls in blasts of silver bolts*
> *Electric fireworks*

And on one January day, these lines emerged:

> *Candle, lamp, and coat*
> *Snuggle me with light and warmth*
> *Kettle steam breathes hope*

Mary Oliver's poetry also goaded me to notice those around me who could use a little attention. Her poetry reminded me I need strength and courage to love others, even the unlovely. Especially the unlovely. As I contemplate a better world, I want to take action to practice the Golden Rule as the New Testament verse of Luke 6:31 proclaims: "And as ye would that men should do to you, do ye also to them likewise."

My desire, revealed in a final haiku:

> *Peace lily unfurls*
> *Holds microphone tall and strong*
> *Proclaims love to all*

According to the Oxford English Dictionary, "Cathexis" is defined as the concentration of mental energy on one particular person, idea, or object. Although the word contains some negative or neutral connotations, it also suggests this idea:

When you care about other people's welfare and learning, you begin to accept their differences—even appreciate them.

To Reflect

What do you love about the world around you?

Think of a time you found it easy to accept someone's differences? Or a time when you found it hard? Why was it easy or hard?

36 – My Work Is Loving The World

My Checkered Life: A Marriage Memoir

Chapter 37

When Marian Subscribed to the Hustler Channel

In our marriage, many times I'm the one who needs special care, often with technology. I'm fairly computer savvy for someone I classify as a digital immigrant, not a digital native. I grew up in the era of wall-mounted phones and typewriters. But hasty moves get me in trouble when I'm online. My husband, gifted with forbearance, often bails me out.

Though I'm not a fan of formulaic Hallmark movies, I'm more a wholesome-romance-kind-of-woman than the femme fatale with the handsome hunk featured on the Hustler Channel. My writing includes the literary, poetry, family stories laced with scripture texts, not sex. The scenes of most of my blogposts take place in the kitchen, not the bedroom.

One Saturday late in March I scrutinized my Aunt Ruthie's teenage diary for far too many hours. I needed a change. So, I decided to zone out with a movie. Maybe I could find one on the Paramount channel, I thought. Guessing the three channel numbers for a movie as I punched in the channel, my eyes nearly fell out of their sockets. On my way to find entertainment, I must have scrambled three numbers for Paramount and landed on a sex-saturated site. Oh, my blessed word! I was horrified. Horrified and erratic, I panicked. "I have to get out of this and quick!" Apparently, my fat fingers flew too fast to change channels. So, instead of pressing the back button, as I intended, I must have clicked Okay.

37 – When Marian Subscribed to the Hustler Channel

"OKAY? NO-NO! It's NOT okay! I fumbled some more and sealed my fate ending up with a 6-hour $16.41 + tax subscription to lurid bedroom scenes.

The Damage

Now I have to get my husband involved. I can't call or "chat" with our internet/TV provider because I'm not listed as primary user on the account. Cliff has to authorize changes. I can't fix the error myself.

Thus begins Cliff's challenge to contact Comcast. He begins with a nine-minute conversation with one agent, who assures him that he will solicit the help of another agent. "Expect a return call, so you can get a refund," the rep assures him.

The call never comes.

Soon after, Cliff makes another futile attempt. Five times he is hung up on. Finally, he yells, "Cancel service!" which gets a rise out of someone at the other end. At last, he speaks to a *live* person for twenty-three minutes. Friendly and cooperative, this rep initiates a refund.

Mennonite girls don't like to be a bother. Not even *former* Mennonite girls. Cliff spent his precious time righting a wrong not even his fault. Bless him!

The Upshot

I am a married woman who has birthed two children. Forsooth, as an English major, I know the contents of Nabokov's *Lolita* and Salinger's *Catcher in the Rye*. I am no prude. Nevertheless, Playboy bunnies and casual coquettes are not my thing. And so, I contemplate safeguards to avoid future snafus. Maybe we should banish the TV all together. Some people get along just fine without a television in the house. I certainly didn't grow up with one.

In retrospect, I could have used the "audio" feature to find the channel I intended. "Audio" would have even succeeded in changing the channels when I first saw my mistake, but that's all water under the bridge now.

Yes, indeed, my husband is a reliable help, though I hope never to petition his help for a channel snafu again!

To Reflect

Have you had to solicit help from someone else who wasn't even part of the problem?

37 – When Marian Subscribed to the Hustler Channel

My Checkered Life: A Marriage Memoir

Chapter 38

Compensation: A Wedding Anniversary Meditation

The "Help" works both ways though in our marriage. We compensate for one another's weaknesses with our own strengths. John Milton asserts that the complementary aspect of marriage makes for a "cheerful and apt conversation," according to one of his tracts on marriage and divorce.

Take a lesson from the animal kingdom. How is a married couple like a herd of African *wildebeests* and zebras? Zoologists know that herds of African wildebeests and zebras migrate together because their strengths compensate for their weaknesses, making them more compatible and less vulnerable to attack. Wildebeests (also called gnus) have poor eyesight, but they have a keen sense of smell, whereas zebras have good eyesight and a poor sense of smell.

Each species has its unique set of qualities to benefit the other. Traveling together, they can fend off enemies who threaten their survival. Like the yin-yang symbol, the two breeds of animals are complementary. *Much like in a good marriage . . .*

In our marriage, I'm the "wildebeest" struggling with poor eyesight, yet I have bionic ears (thanks to my mother's genes).

38 – Compensation: A Wedding Anniversary Meditation

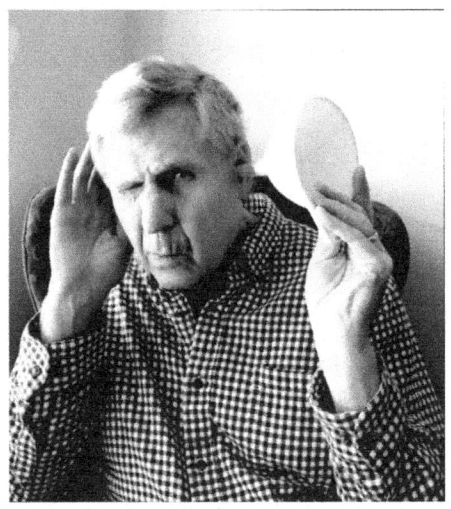

Cliff is hearing impaired but sharp-eyed, a good thing because he is a visual artist.

We compensate in other ways too as this chart illustrates.

He	*Me*
Artist	Writer
Even-tempered	Excitable
Night owl	Chipper in the morning
Inborn GPS	Directionally challenged
Can tolerate "messy"	Loves order
Intuitively able to fix things	Not!
"Reads" audio books	Prefers print

Accommodation, another hefty "-tion" word, is a first cousin to compensation and, practiced often, a boon to harmony.

As the story goes, my Uncle Clyde Metzler, a pastor who officiated at many weddings at Hernley Mennonite Church near Manheim, Pennsylvania, told the starry-eyed couple before they stood at the marriage altar, "There are two bears in your marriage: Bear and forbear. Remember that!" Of course, such wisdom would be true for relationships of all kinds. Some examples:

- *Give your partner the bigger piece of chicken or lemon meringue pie.*

- *Stifle words of contempt. You can't take them back. Find another way to express yourself.*

- *Take a walk.*

- *Get some sleep. Maybe you're just tired and need rest.*

Having shared values helps us as a couple function better when we encounter problems.

I Corinthians 12:6 "There are many ways in which God works in our lives, but it is the same God who does the work in and through all of us who are His."
~ The Living Bible

38 – Compensation: A Wedding Anniversary Meditation

In the year 2020, the year the pandemic began, we celebrated 53 years of marriage. Like every other couple, we have lived through tough times and have had our share of ups and downs. Nevertheless, my husband is still the one I would choose to be quarantined with.

My Checkered Life: A Marriage Memoir

Chapter 39

Standing on the Promises: A Golden Anniversary

A few years ago, we celebrated our fiftieth anniversary, a time to reminisce about our wedding day. On Saturday, August 5, 1967, Cliff and I stood before the pastor of Calvary Presbyterian Church in Charlotte, North Carolina and pledged our troth with words adapted from The Book of Common Prayer.

One of our wedding cards, silvery, rang a clear bell of promise, this one from my oldest cousin Dotty Metzler Martin and her husband Ervin.

In 2017, we celebrated our Golden Anniversary. After fifty years, we are still standing. But not alone then or now.

We stood with our witnesses

My sisters Jean and Janice at left; Cliff's sister Joyce on right; groomsman Don Chapman; my father Ray Longenecker and best man Paul Mumma; and groomsman James Fairfield.

39 – Standing on the Promises: A Golden Anniversary

We stood with friends

Friends and family from Lancaster County, Pennsylvania, drove the long distance that hot August weekend from Pennsylvania Dutch-land to Charlotte, North Carolina. I have recently reviewed their signatures in our wedding guest book, a heart-warming and nostalgic look back. Mennonite or fancy folks, we appreciated their support of our union.

We stood with parents

My parents traveled from Elizabethtown, Pennsylvania, apparently happy their oldest daughter had chosen Cliff as her groom. Cliff's parents and sisters Joyce and Kathy took a northern route in a camper all the way from Washington state, a distance of over twenty-seven hundred miles.

Standing Tall in All Sorts of Weather

This from an essay *On Marriage,* Theodor Gottliebe von Hippel dated 1772:

> *"If a man could receive the advantages of marriage without the duty of standing day and night at a woman's side in all sorts of wind and weather, then nobody would hesitate to get married."*

Why I Married You

"I married you because you gave me a promise. That promise made up for your faults. And the promise I gave you made up for mine. Two imperfect people got married and it was the promise that made the marriage."
– Mrs. Antrobus in Thornton Wilder's *The Skin of Our Teeth*

Leah Furnas remarks in her article, "The Longly-Weds Know," that it isn't about the Golden Anniversary at all but about all the unremarkable years that Hallmark doesn't even make a card for."

39 – Standing on the Promises: A Golden Anniversary

My Checkered Life: A Marriage Memoir

Chapter 40

Marriage on the Rocks

> "There is nothing more admirable than when two people who see eye to eye keep house as man and wife, confounding their enemies and delighting their friends."
>
> ~ Homer, The Odyssey

The House Ways and Means Committee

For more than **55 years** now, Cliff and I have been co-chairs of our House Ways and Means Committee.

- We find *ways* to live within our *means*.

- We try to avoid being *mean* in spite of disparate *ways* of viewing the world, he being from Mars and I from Venus.

- In conversation, we find *ways* to figure out what each other *means*.

The Flashing Fish of Hope from "A Pretty Sweet Thing"

"No long-term marriage is made easily, and there have been times when I've been so angry or so hurt that I thought my love would never recover. And then, in the midst of near despair, something has happened beneath the surface. A bright little flashing fish of hope has flicked silver fins and the water is bright and suddenly I am returned to a state of love again . . . . I've learned that there will always be a next time, and that I will submerge in darkness and misery, but that I won't stay submerged . . . . The best I can ask for is that this love, which has been built on countless failures, will continue to grow. I can say no more than that this is mystery, and gift, and that somehow or other, through grace, our failures can be redeemed and blessed."
~ Madeleine l'Engle, "A Pretty Sweet Thing"

"You're just tired!"

Emma was chopping vegetables for a stir-fry when Chris came home from work one night looking tired and stressed. When she asked him about his day, he just groaned.

Chris started thumbing through the mail . . . and found a VISA bill that showed that Emma had spent more than $100 on meals out with Alice and the twins. "I'm not made of money," he grumbled.

Although she was tempted to snap at him, Emma had been married for a long time. She knew this wasn't about the money, but about his day. She stopped chopping and walked over to him. She gave him a hand squeeze and said, "Oh, honey, I'm sorry you had a bad day." ~ Mary Pipher, *Women Rowing North*

Author friend and blogger Elaine Mansfield also admits to having a full-blown argument with her husband Vic, which she records in a post, "The Art of Argument, Essential Marriage Skills 101." Elaine spells out the details of an argument that ensued when her husband made a decision to respond to an invitation without consulting her. Theirs was not a fatal argument either, nor was it a final one, but her story reveals the art of restraint and more, especially at the brink. The incident also hints at eventual reconciliation.

Since the Golden Wedding Anniversary, we've had our own share of conflicts, rare but recurring. The texture of our life together is checkered, never bland. Tiredness, misunderstandings with our grown children, and deadlines are often the culprits. Just last weekend we had a blow-up. I became a simmering tea kettle with a head of steam that eventually screamed, "You make me so mad!" An income tax deadline loomed, our son, who promised to change switches on the outdoor fountain, didn't show up as we expected, and plans for our oldest grandsons' farewell breakfast were up in the air. Twin factors, physical exhaustion and too-high expectations, thickened the air like purple clouds roiling before a thunderstorm.

One recurring event that causes tension is the protracted income tax preparation for two self-employed mates, one an artist, the other a writer. Methodical Cliff uses Excel spreadsheets.

I say, "Golly, you sure use a lot of color on these forms!"

"Yep, that's how I know how to separate our expenses—yours and mine—and calculate income."

Income tax due and grandkids leaving for college

In my writing studio, the flame on my cinnamon-scented candle flickers, the tongue of fire recalling a flare-up last Sunday evening.

"We have to settle this *now*. I don't want to go to bed mad!" Cliff says, sitting on the edge of the blue bed spread in our guest room where I have been snacking and stewing alone. He wants to get things straightened out after an argument, while I like to simmer before we decide to get back on the same page again.

"Stop with this nonsense," I yelled earlier. "You have enough figures to file that stupid IRS report for 2021."

40 – Marriage on the Rocks

Cliff yelled back, mimicking my volume but in a lower register. I paused, surprised at his loud response, "See how you like that!" Then he pressed on, "I have to get it right. I can't fudge on figures! I must substantiate every expense. I don't want to trigger another audit. You don't understand." I stomped off to my writing studio, he scooted back to his refuge in his corner red chair and ottoman to listen to his audio book, Clive Cussler's *Dark Vector*.

Our tiff was tipped off by an accumulation of grievances mingled with fatigue: mis-communication with our children about meeting up to say farewell to two freshman grandsons going off to the University of Florida and Cliff's obsessive-compulsive zeal for a "perfect" income-tax filing with itemized deductions. "You spend too much time on useless detail. Mike (our accountant) says too many business deductions may trigger an income tax audit."

We'd been through an audit twice: once in the 1990s when an IRS agent came to our house, suspicious that our home office for Cliff's graphic arts business may be a front for drug dealing. "Drug dealing, for heaven's sake. That's absurd!" I struck back. The woman peeked into our closets, looking for evidence. Amazingly, in the end, it turned out the IRS owed *us* money because of a newly initiated tax credit for vehicles, a deduction that Cliff wasn't aware of.

The second time, we were summoned to the Federal Building in downtown Jacksonville just before our trip to Ukraine in 2011. The agent, suited in brown plaid with a white turtleneck that obviously choked off blood supply, glared at us. She moved with sloth-liked fingers, prolonging the agony. Try to picture Flash the Sloth in the Disney movie Zootopia but without the comedy. Cliff had previously filed IRS reports himself, putting some figures in the wrong slots and claiming roof "cost" not "depreciation," a tag acceptable over a longer period of time. Our newly-hired accountant, Intercessor Irene, stepped in to get penalty and interest charges removed. Honestly, I don't remember a huge blast to our budget over the whole ordeal.

Cliff as Cartoonist is usually laid-back, prone to generating squiggly lines in caricature and impromptu innuendo as jokester. However, with the IRS, his artistic flair mutates into reams of Excel spreadsheets, his Tailor-made Tax Organizer with rectilinear entries, shot with color, delineating income sources: Pink for Marian the writer, Orange for Cliff the artist, Yellow for sub-columns, Blue for totals, and Green for rows of categories.

Since the beginning of our marriage, both our incomes funnel into one pot. We usually discuss larger items. Cliff needing a $300.00 eight-terabyte storage drive for huge visual files gets my okay. He never fusses over big drains like my cataract surgery costing $5000.00, even with supplemental insurance. "It's worth it. You can't put a price tag on good vision," he assures me. I pay our bills online and write out the odd bank check for piano tuning or extra charitable giving. Cliff keeps up with the monthly Quicken accounts, adapting the data for yearly income tax reports.

40 – Marriage on the Rocks

Last week's argument finally did get settled. Cliff waved his hand toward me with a quick salute, clearing the air, "Okay, things are level now." We got rest for our exhausted bodies and later leaned into a familiar, friendly rhythm. I hate it when we clash, though, the conflict seeping into my soul like stain into thick fabric, woven into our checkered life. Still, the sun, that star of fiery love, helps bleach out the blotch, so we can move forward.

This title, Marriage on the Rocks, is both a pun and a teaser. In the photo above, we were sitting on the coquina "rock" of the Old Fort Castillo de San Marcos in St. Augustine, Florida, our first stop of a day-trip getaway! As far as I can tell, our marriage has not yet hit the rocks! **The truth is, our marriage is built on The Rock,** a shared faith in God's power to hold us together, especially in tough times.

> *Lead me to the Rock that is higher than I.*
> *– Psalm 61:3*

> *The LORD is my rock, and my fortress, and my deliverer; my God, my strength, in whom I will trust: my buckler, and the horn of my salvation, and my high tower.*
> *– Psalm 18:2*

I am thinking now of the prayer the minister prayed as we knelt before the altar and beside each other so many years ago. (from The Book of Common Prayer)

> *Bless them and develop their characters as they walk together with You. Give them enough hurts to keep them humane, enough failures to keep their hands clenched tightly in Yours, and enough of success to make them sure they walk with You throughout all of their life.*

> *May they never take each other's love for granted but always experience that breathless wonder that exclaims, "Out of all this world, you have chosen me." Then, when life is done and the sun is setting, may they be found then as now, still hand in hand, still very proud, still thanking You for each other.*

40 – Marriage on the Rocks

May they travel together as friends and lovers, brother and sister, husband and wife, father and mother, and as servants of Christ until He shall return or until that day when one shall lay the other into the arms of God. This we ask through Jesus Christ, our Lord and Savior, the Great Lover of our souls. Amen.

The God who knit us together

in our mother's womb, separate and wholly different human beings, according to Psalm 139:13 (New Living Translation), has over time bound us together in both heart and spirit, the two becoming one.

My Checkered Life: A Marriage Memoir

A Final Tribute

This prayer reminds me of a tribute to my husband enclosed in a letter I wrote to another pastor in 2009 after we had been married almost forty-two years. His message, referring to challenges inherent in marriage, prompted me to write this homage to Cliff and also as an encouragement to our pastor:

Dear Pastor,

You probably hear more reports of the marriages in trouble rather than harmonious ones, so I thought you would welcome some good news for a change. My husband Cliff is a master at marital communication. He listens! My only indication that I am including too much detail or going on for too long is that he begins to smile. He constantly scans my facial expression to access my EQ (emotional quotient). During the day, he calls me to see how my day is going and lets me know when he'll be home.

During the nineties, when he was traveling extensively with his art shows, he would send me audio tapes, a collage of words and music that expressed his creativity and let me know that he missed me. I suppose too it was his way of staying out of trouble on the road.

Cliff would agree with me that neatness is not his strong suit, but when he is home, I can count on him to make the bed in the morning—even change sheets. Although he has an extremely busy schedule, he makes sure that things are running smoothly in the household; he has initiated several remodeling projects.

When we discuss our journey together, he tells me that early on he asked God for wisdom to be a good husband and made a conscious decision to stick with it. Only he and I know how hard it has been—and how rewarding!

With appreciation,

Marian Beaman

My Checkered Life: A Marriage Memoir

Epilogue

Mennonite women with white prayer caps. A quilting frame with fabric stretched taut. Checkered designs often with colors more flamboyant than the clothes they wore. From my early years, the word "quilt" has evoked Mennonite women around a quilting frame, following treasured designs, seldom deviating from a pattern.

Long ago, my mother, Ruth Longenecker, and grandma Fannie quilted with other women of Bossler Mennonite Church near Elizabethtown, Pennsylvania, in a schoolhouse turned into sewing space beside the church. Their work was fine, their needles sharp, their stitches small. With nimble fingers, they worked on a rectangular table or a quilting frame, stitching comfort for needy souls while sharing stories. They usually followed strict patterns but sometimes individual quilters made patchwork quilts from what is regarded as a "pile-up of possibilities," putting fabric remnants to good use.

Quilts these days can express more flexible patterns. One I've seen resembles coin-shaped eucalyptus leaves placed at odd angles, or another imitating spaghetti-like scribbles like in a Jackson Pollock painting. Depending on one's taste, both can be beautiful.

The quilt displayed on my book cover is merely a quilt top, a gift from my mother, Ruth Metzler Longenecker. I display it on top

My Checkered Life: A Marriage Memoir

of our bedspread sometimes "just for pretty." I enjoy the design and the love it still summons, but the quilt itself is incomplete as a sewing project.

To finish the quilt as a blanket or a wall hanging, I would have to add batting and a backing. Batting, the cushiony layer between the quilt top and the backing, adds structure and warmth. The backing, cut two inches larger than the original top, is placed under the batting, and quilt top. Then the batting and backing are quilted together. YouTube offers several good demos of this process. I want to finish the quilt, so when I pass it on to the next generation, it can be usable as a blanket or even a piece of wall art. It begs to be completed, a tangible piece of history from my mother handed down to my children and grandchildren.

Author Linda Lipsett researched the lives of seven New England crafters, women who created signature quilts. She dug through public records and traveled across America interviewing genealogists and descendants of the women whose quilts she owned, most created in the 1840s and 1850s. In her book, *Remember Me: Women and their Friendship Quilts*, Lipsett underscores the fact that "It was not a woman's desire to be forgotten. And in one simple, unpretentious way, she created a medium that would outlive even many of her husband's houses, barns and fences; she signed her name in friendship onto cloth and, in her own way, cried out, Remember me!"

The author goes on to suggest that there is "a sense of permanence that permeates" the folds of a quilt.

My Checkered Life: A Marriage Memoir

Memorial services for quilters have sometimes echoed the sentiment of remembrance. Children and grandchildren of the loved one have displayed quilts over the back of pews at the funeral, a visual demonstration of how the quilter communicated love for her family, leaving her own signature to posterity.

I am not a quilter. My checkered life is not about sewing, though I made my plain Mennonite dresses with capes, fashioned a fancy *peau de soie* wedding gown with a lace jacket. Later I made pale blue batiste living room drapes with pinch pleats for our first home. The checkered life I've lived includes a motley mélange of moments, a patchwork of vignettes: the burnished bronze of two disparate families, the Beamans and the Longeneckers, merging the blues of life in a tiny trailer, the blinking orange of dangers in London and Positano, and, through the years, the Cupid red of enduring love.

Whether you are a quilter, a gardener, a writer, or fit another special niche, you probably aspire to create something meaningful and lasting with your life, leaving a legacy. Don't we all want to know that our lives have meant something? That though we may be gone, we are not forgotten.

Epilogue

References

Introduction

Otto, Whitney. "How to Make an American Quilt." New York: Penguin Random House. 1991. Movie adaptation. October 6, 1995.

Heritage and Home

Auden, W. H. "Musée des Beaux Arts," lines 14-21, 1940. http://english.emory.edu/classes/paintings&poems/auden.html

Beaman, Marian L. Mennonite Daughter: The Story of a Plain Girl. Jacksonville, Florida: Spindletree Books, 2019.

Berry, Wendell. "On Poetry and Marriage" https://www.firstthings.com/blogs/firstthoughts/2013/01/wendell-berrys-changed-mind-on-marriage

Marital Happiness and Hassles

Calhoun, Ada. "Wedding Toasts I'll Never Give" https://www.goodreads.com/book/show/32051305-wedding-toasts-i-ll-never-give?ac=1&from_search=true

"It's not easy being green" https://www.youtube.com/watch?v=rRZ-IxZ46ng&ab_channel=JayB7869

"Where's My Spyglass?"
http://simplyorderly.com/surprising-statistics/

Hilarity and High Emotion

Cision website:
https://www.prnewswire.com/news-releases/lost-and-found-the-average-american-spends-25-days-each-year-looking-for-lost-items-collectively-costing-us-households-27-billion-annually-in-replacement-costs-300449305.html

"The Story Behind the Dollar Bill" Events occurring in 1962:
https://en.wikipedia.org/wiki/April_1962

Harmony in Marriage and in Life

Cohen, Leonard. "Dance Me to the End of Love."
https://www.azlyrics.com/lyrics/leonardcohen/anthem.html

Elrod, Hal, quotation: "Are You Too Big for Your Pot?"
https://www.azquotes.com/author/64218-Hal_Elrod

Lamott, Anne. *Stitches: A Handbook of Meaning, Hope, and Repair.* New York: Riverhead Books, 2013.

"Morning Ablutions: What's Your Routine?"
https://www.hellopeacefulmind.com/why-you-need-a-morning-routine/

References

Morning Routines, historical figures: Ben Franklin, Victor Hugo, and Jens Christian's "Grøndahl"
https://taylorpearson.me/morning/

Oliver, Mary. "My Work is Loving the World."
https://www.awakin.org/v2/read/view.php?tid=2168

Sandburg, Carl. "Smoke and Steel."
Easter Meditation with Jonah and Carl Sandburg.
https://www.bartleby.com/231/0408.html

Story of Jonah:
https://www.biblegateway.com/passage/?search=Jonah+2%3B2&version=OJB,
Orthodox Jewish Bible

"Why Creating a Meaningful Morning Routine Will Make You More Successful."
https://www.huffpost.com/entry/morning-routines_b_8042428

Compensation: A Wedding Anniversary Meditation

Snow Africa Adventure:
https://snowafricaadventure.com/blog/why-do-zebra-and-wildebeest-migrate-together/

Standing on the Promises: A Golden Anniversary

Furnas, Leah. "The Longly-Weds Know."
https://allpoetry.com/poem/3571202-The-Longly-weds-Know-by-XxEmOtiOnjOxX

Gottliebe von Hippel. "On Marriage." 1772
https://searchworks.stanford.edu/view/2873624

Wilder, Thornton. The Skin of Our Teeth.
https://www.goodreads.com/quotes/189598

Marriage on the Rocks

L'Engle, Madeleine. "A Pretty Sweet Thing."
https://en.wikiquote.org/wiki/Madeleine_L%27Engle

Pipher, Mary. "Women Rowing North."
New York: Bloomsbury Publishing, 2019.

References

Epilogue

Bechtold, Peggy. "Meaning Mondays: Life as a Quilt Edition." April 19, 2010. https://livingdeepstudio.com/2010/04/19/meaning-mondays-life-as-a-quilt-edition/

Lipsett, Linda Otto. "Remember Me: Women & Their Friendship Quilts." San Francisco: The Quilt Digest Press. January 1, 1985.

Lipsett, Linda Otto. "Remember Me: Women & Their Friendship Quilts." https://www.amazon.com/Remember-Me-Women-Friendship-Quilts/dp/0913327174/ref=sr_1_2?dchild=1&keywords=Remember+Me+Linda+Otto+Lipsett&qid=1632149290&s=books&sr=1-2

My Checkered Life: A Marriage Memoir

Acknowledgements

Writing is a solitary endeavor, but publishing a book requires a devoted team. I am indebted to these fine authors whom I am happy to call friends: early readers Sally Constain and Anni Rawcliffe of Riverwood Writes and Colleen McConnell, my ideal reader. Authors who supplied their editing skills include Susan Weidener, developmental editing; Melodie Miller Davis, beta reading/editing, and Liesbet Collaert, copyediting. I am also appreciative of other friends who provided endorsements for this book: Laurie Buchanan, Melodie Miller Davis, Shirley Hershey Showalter, Elfrieda Shroeder, and Pamela Wight. And, finally, to designer Stockton Eller, for invaluable assistance in bringing this book to publication.

I am grateful for the patterns for living both my husband and I learned from our forebears: strong work ethic, persistence, and faithfulness in marriage. Special thanks to my partner in life and the topic of many of these stories, my companion Clifford Dean Beaman. I couldn't have chosen a better helpmate.

My Checkered Life: A Marriage Memoir

I hope you enjoyed reading this book

May I ask you a favor?

Like all authors, I rely on online reviews to encourage future sales. Your opinion is valuable. Will you take a few minutes to record your assessment of my book on Amazon, Goodreads, or any other book review website you prefer. Your review needn't be long: Sometimes 3-5 sentences can be effective.

Your opinion will help the book marketplace become more transparent and useful to everyone.

Thank you very much!

My Checkered Life: A Marriage Memoir

About the Author

Award-winning teacher turned story teller, Marian Beaman is enjoying her encore career as a writer. A former college professor, the author records the charms and challenges of growing up plain in mid-twentieth century Pennsylvania in *Mennonite Daughter: The Story of a Plain Girl.* This memoir tells the story of her transformation from a provincial young woman in a sheltered environment who finds her authentic self. Along the way, she discovers a path toward forgiveness of childhood abuse. She also shows how one's growth can include respect for the past.

My Checkered Life: A Marriage Memoir takes an intimate look into one couple's fifty-plus-year marriage. Using a quilt motif, the author stitches together stories that make up the fabric of their daily lives: the clash of cultures, crisis in a travel trailer, surviving a robbery, and enduring financial hardship. Readers can observe how they find common ground through their shared faith and commitment. This sequel includes curated diary entries and treasured recipes. The author blogs regularly at marianbeaman.com

My Checkered Life: A Marriage Memoir

About the Artist

Cliff Beaman, who holds a master's degree from Florida State University, has enjoyed a varied career as both artist and educator. Early on, he developed an art assembly program entitled The History of Art, performed in schools throughout southeastern United States. As a graphic artist, he designed corporate logos and used his cartooning skills to create training programs for various businesses. For more than three decades, his multi-media art assembly programs, American Art Assemblies, have inspired young people across the nation with educational themes created on an easel, accompanied by exciting music and special lighting effects. You can find video clips and descriptions of Cliff's performances at americanartassemblies.com

Cliff as storyteller has written and illustrated The Boy Who Grew Too Small and created art work for several other authors. He has provided special artistic designs for his wife Marian's blog posts, along with illustrations for both of her memoirs, *Mennonite Daughter* and *My Checkered Life*. The couple resides in Jacksonville, Florida.

My Checkered Life: A Marriage Memoir